Cyril Davenport

The English Regalia

Cyril Davenport

The English Regalia

ISBN/EAN: 9783337777609

Printed in Europe, USA, Canada, Australia, Japan

Cover: Foto ©Thomas Meinert / pixelio.de

More available books at **www.hansebooks.com**

THE ENGLISH REGALIA

THE ENGLISH REGALIA

BY CYRIL DAVENPORT

LONDON
KEGAN PAUL, TRENCH, TRÜBNER
AND COMPANY, LIMITED
1897

THE ENGLISH REGALIA

BY CYRIL DAVENPORT

F.S.A.

LONDON
KEGAN PAUL, TRENCH, TRÜBNER
AND COMPANY, LIMITED
1897

TO HER
MOST GRACIOUS MAJESTY
VICTORIA
OF GREAT BRITAIN AND IRELAND
QUEEN
EMPRESS OF INDIA
THIS BOOK IS BY SPECIAL PERMISSION
DEDICATED
BY HER LOYAL AND FAITHFUL
SUBJECT AND SERVANT
THE AUTHOR

CORONATION DAY
JUNE 28TH, 1897

PREFACE

N the summer of 1896 I was allowed, by Her Majesty's gracious permission, to examine and photograph the Regalia out of their cases, and without this privilege it would have been impossible to obtain plates of the excellence and reliability of those illustrating this work, as the light in the Jewel House is most unfavourable.

I am also much indebted to the two Keepers of the Regalia who have been the victims of my search after knowledge. General Sir Michael A. S. Biddulph, G.C.B., himself an admirable artist, and his successor, Lieut.-General Sir Frederick D. Middleton, K.C.M.G., C.B., have both most patiently and courteously given me every facility in their power, as well for my photographs as for my sketches, and indeed I believe they have both taken a personal interest in my researches into the history and the details of the decoration of the treasures intrusted to their care.

On the occasion of my seeing the Regalia out of their cases I obtained permission to take with me Mr. William Griggs, as I mistrusted my own powers as a photographer, and was anxious to reap the full advantage of the rare occasion and get the best negatives possible. Mr. Griggs succeeded better than I had expected; but nevertheless much artistic work has been necessary in addition, in order to produce the plates in the present book. I feel that I owe Mr. Griggs many thanks for the patience with which he has listened to my various suggestions, and for the skill with which he has carried them out; and I trust that our united labours may have produced illustrations of the Regalia as they now are which may some day have an historic value beyond the artistic one which alone can be claimed for them to-day.

The small illustrations in the text are made from drawings of my own, and they will, I hope, make the subject-matter clearer than it

THE ENGLISH REGALIA

otherwise would be; more especially in the inquiry into the growth of the form of the crown I think they are necessary for the clear understanding of the case.

With regard to Her Majesty's vestments, I am indebted to Mr. Arnold Royle, C.B., the Keeper of the Robes, for his kind permission to examine them and make pictorial notes.

I have consulted all the books concerning the Regalia that I could find, but I do not profess in any way to have gone into the large question of the origin and history of our coronation ceremonies—that inquiry is already in very good hands. I have examined carefully only such books as deal with the details of the insignia of Royalty in England. Many times I have thought I had found new forms of early crowns in old manuscripts, but unfortunately on a little further examination they have turned out to be only imaginations of the mediæval artist.

The books that I have found of most value, and which I have freely made use of, are—

> The *Liber Regalis*, at Westminster.
> Rymer's *Fœdera*.
> Sir Edward Walker's *The Preparations for His Maiestie's Coronation at Westminster, the 23rd of Aprill* 1661. MS.
> John Ogilvy. *The Entertainment of His Most Excellent Majestie Charles II.*, etc. London, 1662.
> Francis Sandford. *The History of the Coronation of the Most High Monarch James II.*, etc. In the Savoy, 1687.
> *The Ceremonial of the Coronation of His Most Sacred Majesty King George the Fourth.* [By Sir George Nayler, Garter King of Arms.] Westminster, 1823.
> William Jones. *Crowns and Coronations.* London, 1883.
> William Chaffers. *Gilda Aurifabrorum,* a History of English Goldsmiths, etc. London, 1883.
> J. Wickham Legg. *The Sacring of the English Kings,* etc. London, 1894.

My sketches of details from the Great Seals I have generally taken from the Seals themselves; but I have checked my own observations by reference to the admirable book on the Great Seals of England by Alfred B. Wyon, completed by Allan Wyon. London, 1887.

The drawings from the coins are in many cases from the coins

PREFACE

themselves; but I have in this point found much assistance from Rogers Ruding's *Annals of the Coinage of Britain*, etc. London, 1819.

I also gratefully acknowledge the kindness of Lord Amherst of Hackney, who readily allowed me to examine and sketch the curious settings of old English state crowns which now belong to him.

CYRIL DAVENPORT.

TABLE OF CONTENTS

	PAGE
Preface	vii
Historical Introduction	1
Vestments	14
Orbs	17
Sceptres	19
Crowns	21
The Ampulla	28
The Spoon	30
Queen Elizabeth's Salt-Cellar	32
St. Edward's Crown	34
The Royal Sceptre with the Cross	35
The Queen's Sceptre with the Cross	36
The Larger Orb	37
The Sceptre with the Dove	38
The Queen's Sceptre with the Dove	39
The Smaller Orb	40
St. Edward's Staff	41
The Queen's Ivory Rod	41
Bracelets	42
Queen Mary of Modena's Circlet	44
Queen Mary of Modena's Crown	45

TABLE OF CONTENTS

	PAGE
The Prince of Wales's Coronet	46
Swords	47
Spurs	48
Queen Victoria's State Crown	50
The Mace, Banqueting Plate, etc.	52
The Coronation Book	55
The Koh-i-noor	57
St. Edward's Chair	60
Index	63

LIST OF COLOURED PLATES

PLATE.	DESCRIPTION.	TO FACE PAGE
1.	The Ampulla	28
2.	The Coronation Spoon Queen Elizabeth's Salt-Cellar	30
3.	St. Edward's Crown	34
4.	The Royal Sceptre with the Cross The Larger Orb The Queen's Sceptre with the Cross	36
5.	The Sceptre with the Dove The Smaller Orb The Queen's Sceptre with the Dove	38
6.	The Queen's Ivory Rod The Bracelets St. Edward's Staff	42
7.	The Circlet of Queen Mary of Modena	44
8.	The State Crown of Queen Mary of Modena	45
9.	The Coronet of the Prince of Wales	46
10.	The Sword of State St. George's Spurs The Sword 'Curtana'	48
11.	Queen Victoria's State Crown	50
12.	Head of Mace of Charles II.	52

THE ENGLISH REGALIA

HERE are many authorities for the order of the coronations in England, to be found at the British Museum, in the Bodleian Library at Oxford, and in the muniment-room at Westminster Abbey, and in all material points they resemble each other very closely. From the time of Æthelred II., in the tenth century, down to the latest coronation, the leading features have been the anointing, the vesting, the crowning, and the presentation of the sceptre; and it is remarkable also that in most of these ceremonials there is mention of a second or state crown. The most concise and complete account of the ceremony of coronation is, I think, to be found in a little vellum manuscript now preserved in the muniment-room at Westminster Abbey, and known as the *Liber Regalis*. The order given in this book is supposed to have been used at the coronation of Richard II., although it is probably a compilation from an earlier manuscript, and appears to have been written about 1350. The order generally, as given in the *Liber Regalis*, is, after certain preliminary formalities—

The Anointing.

Then after much delay and careful ablutions, which were very elaborate and tedious, came the vesting with the royal garments—

1. The Colobium Sindonis, always a simple linen garment.
2. The Tunicle or Dalmatic, described as 'Tunica talaris cum ymaginibus, cum caligis, sandariis et calcaribus,' *i.e.*
3. Shoes, buskins and spurs. Then comes
4. The Sword, and
5. The Stole or Armilla, 'iste quidem armille in modum stole circa collum et ab utraque scapula usque ad compages brachiorum erunt dependentes,' from which it appears that the stole was not worn crossed but hanging straight down on each side.
6. The Imperial Mantle, 'Pallium regale quadrum cum aquilis aureis.' These eagles have retained their place on the imperial mantle ever since, but they are described as of gold, whereas now they are silver;

THE ENGLISH REGALIA

and although the Dalmatic is said to have had designs upon it, there is no detailed mention of them.

Next the sovereign is endued with the actual emblems of royalty,

1. The Crown;
2. The Ring;
3. The Sceptres.

There are two kinds of sceptres mentioned : the first with a cross, to be held in the right hand, ' Deinde dabitur ei sceptrum in manu dextra, quod quidem sceptrum aureum est, in cujus summitate crux parua collocatur.' The other, bearing a dove, is to be held in the left hand, ' Post modum tradatur ei uirga in manu sinistra, que quidem uirga aurea est habens in summitate columbam auream '; and it is interesting to note that in Sir George Hayter's picture of the coronation of Queen Victoria, she is represented as holding both these sceptres exactly in this manner, the only important difference being that the dove at the top of the sceptre in her left hand is white instead of gold as described. The *Liber Regalis* has three full-page illustrations, but I think that not much reliance can be placed on any of the representations of the regalia which occur in illuminated manuscripts, as it was of course perfectly easy for the illuminator to follow his own fancy, which he undoubtedly often did. Indeed, even when former coronations are described and illustrated, the mediæval artists having no idea of antiquarian accuracy, and apparently having made no effort in this direction, at the best their illustrations would only serve as indications of the fashion of the actual time when they were written.

In the ceremony of coronation the double character of the sovereign is shown very clearly—the priestly character, however, preponderating over the military. The ceremonies of the anointing and the sequence of prayers used closely resemble the procedure at the consecration of a bishop, and the vestments are, if not quite the same, at least analogous to those worn by a bishop. The 'colobium sindonis' may be taken for the alb or rochet, the 'dalmatic' is common to both, as are the 'stole' and the ring; and the imperial mantle, 'four square,' takes the place of the cope. The sceptre corresponds to the crozier, and the crown to the mitre. The orb alone, which has been used by all our kings since Edward the Confessor, appears, so far as I can trace, to stand quite alone as an emblem of independent sovereignty, and has nothing to do with either priest or soldier.

The military emblems are the sword and spurs. In all the earlier coronation ceremonies smaller insignia were also used; the most important of these were the buskins, the sandals, and the gloves, but they have now more or less fallen into disuse.

In the time of Edward the Confessor the regalia, together with the

THE ENGLISH REGALIA

other royal treasures, were kept in Westminster Abbey in a small room in the eastern cloister, which was in fact the 'Treasury of England.' The abbot and monks of Westminster, by the authority of the foundation charter of Edward the Confessor, had charge of the regalia and coronation robes; but this responsibility must frequently have been a light one, because until comparatively recent times our kings were in the habit of carrying their regalia about with them. It may be remembered that in 1415 Henry V. wore his crown at Agincourt, and it is said to have saved his life from the Duc D'Alençon, who, however, succeeded in chipping part of it off. Again, Richard III. in 1485 wore his at Bosworth field, on which occasion it was hidden in a hawthorn bush, and found by Sir Reginald Bray. The crown being handy was at once used to crown the Earl of Richmond, who was on the spot proclaimed Henry VII. by Lord Stanley, and in memory of this, he afterwards used as one of his badges a red-berried hawthorn bush, with sometimes a crown in it; and there is an old saying, 'Cleave to the crown, though it hang on a bush.' Although the proper place of deposit for the royal treasure was at Westminster, in times of any special trouble or danger it was sent to the Tower of London for safety. In 1303 the Treasury at Westminster was broken into by a monk, and much damage was done to it and its contents; and after much moving backwards and forwards it was at last considered that at Westminster sufficient care could never be taken of the valuable collection, and the regalia were finally removed to the Tower during the reign of Henry VIII.

In Rymer's *Fœdera* there are numerous lists and inventories of the royal treasure of England, and in the reign of Henry III. for the first time there appears a regularly appointed Keeper of the Regalia. He had precedence next to Privy Councillors, wore a scarlet robe at the coronation, with a crown embroidered on the left shoulder. He dined at the baron's table at Westminster Hall, and had the high privilege of placing the king's crown on his head, and again removing it, at the opening of Parliament.

As might be expected, the Royal Treasury underwent many vicissitudes and spoliations at the hands of several of our kings. If Parliament would not grant supplies, kings still had great treasure that they could rapidly sell or pawn for ready money.

In 1623, when Prince Charles went to Spain to woo the Infanta, it is said that he took from the Tower treasure valued at £600,000. Two years later, when he was king, he fitted out a fleet, under his favourite the Duke of Buckingham, to carry on a war with Spain, and supplies not being forthcoming from Parliament he parted with a large amount of treasure to procure them. The treasure was pawned to Holland, with which country there was an alliance; and the result of the expedition was disastrous, neither does it appear that the treasure was ever redeemed.

THE ENGLISH REGALIA

This was one of the earliest of the troubles between Charles I. and his Parliament.

In 1643 Charles turned the crown and sceptre into money, and in 1644 the Commons ordered the king's plate in the Tower to be melted down and coined. The Lords, to their lasting credit, remonstrated against this, and declared that the workmanship was worth far more than the precious metals; but in 1649 the Commons, whose will of course was paramount, ordered the complete destruction of the regalia, then under the keepership of Sir Harry Mildmay, afterwards called 'the knave of diamonds.'

The list of the regalia, as existing at this time, was printed in *Archæologia*, vol. xv. p. 285, from the original manuscript.

On the 9th of August 1649, it was ordered that the regalia should be delivered to the 'trustees for the sale of the goods of the late king, who are to cause the same to be totally broken, and that they melt down all the gold and silver, and sell the jewels to the best advantage of the Commonwealth.'

The list is as follows :—

'A true and perfect Inventory of all the plate and jewells now being in the upper Jewell-house of the Tower, in the charge of Sir Henry Mildmay, together with an appraisement of them, made and taken the 13th, 14th, and 15th daies of August 1649:

'The Imperial crowne of massy gold, weighing 7 lbs. 6 oz.,
   valued at £1110 0 0
'The queenes crowne of massy gold, weighing 3 lbs. 10 oz., . 338 3 4
'A small crowne found in an iron chest, formerly in the Lord
   Cottington's charge (from other accounts this appears to
   have been the crown of Edward VI.), . . . 73 16 8
'—— the gold, the diamonds, rubies, sapphires, etc., . 355 0 0
'The globe, weighing 1 lb. 5¼ oz., ... 57 10 0
'Two coronation bracelets, weighing 7 oz. (with three rubies
   and twelve pearls), ... 36 0 0
'Two sceptres, weighing 18 oz., ... 60 0 0
'A long rodd of silver gilt, 1 lb. 5 oz., . . . 4 10 8

'The foremention'd crownes, since ye inventorie was taken, are, accordinge to ord^r of parm^t totallie broken and defaced.

'*The inventory of that part of the regalia which are now removed from Westminster Abbey to the Jewel-house in the Tower.*

'Queene Edith's crowne, formerly thought to be of massy gould,
   but, upon trial, found to be of silver gilt; enriched with
   garnetts, foule pearle, saphires and some odd stones, poiz.
   50½ oz., valued at £16 0 0
'King Alfred's crowne of goulde wyer worke, sett with slight
   stones. poiz. 79½ oz., at £3 per oz., . . . 248 10 0

THE ENGLISH REGALIA

'A goulde plate dish, enamelled, etc.,	£77	11	0
'One large glass cupp, wrought in figures, etc.,	102	15	0
'A dove of gould, sett with stones, and pearle, poiz. 8½ oz., in a box sett with studs of silver gilt, .	26	0	0
'The gould and stones belonging to a collar of crimson and taffaty, etc.,	18	15	0
'One staff of black and white ivory, with a dove on the top, with binding and foote of goulde, .	4	10	0
'A large staff with a dove on ye top, formerly thought to be all gould, but upon triall found to be, the lower part wood within and silver gilt without,	2	10	0
'Two scept^{rs} one sett with pearles and stones, the upper end gould, the lower end silver. The other silver gilt with a dove, formerly thought gould, .	65	16	10½
'One silver spoone gilt, poiz. 3 oz.,	0	16	0
'The gould of the tassels of the livor cull'd robe, weighing 4 oz., valued at £8, and the coat with the neck button of gould, £2, the robe having some pearle, valued at £3, in all	13	0	0
'All these according to order of Parliament are broken and defaced.			
'One paire of silver gilt spurres, etc., .	1	13	4'

This list is very interesting, as it shows that there must have been considerable care taken of the ancient regalia, as King Alfred's crown of wire-work is mentioned as well as Queen Edith's; and it must also be noted that there is no mention of the eagle of gold, but that there is mention of a silver spoon.

The ancient coronation robes destroyed at the same time are catalogued and valued as follows:—

'One common taffaty robe, very old, valued at .	£0	10	0
'One robe, laced with goulde lace,	0	10	0
'One livor cull^{nt} silk robe, very old and worth nothing,	0	0	0
'One robe of crimson taffaty, sarcenett valued at	0	5	0
'One paire of buskins, cloth of silver and silver stockings, very old, and valued at .	0	2	6
'One paire of shoes of cloth of gold, at .	0	2	6
'One paire of gloves embroid^{ed} wth gould, at	0	1	0
'Three swords with scabbards of cloth of goulde, at	3	0	0
'One old combe of horne, worth nothing,	0	0	0
Total in the chest,	£4	10	6'

The comb was probably for arranging the hair after the anointing.

In looking at the values of these articles, it must not be forgotten that money was worth much more in the time of the Commonwealth than it is now; but even taking this into consideration, it is evident that in their valuation the officers of the Commonwealth were influenced by a certain dislike to the emblems of royalty.

The coronation of Charles II., after several delays, was eventually

THE ENGLISH REGALIA

celebrated on the 23rd of April 1661, and very probably among the reasons for its postponement was the fact that there were no regalia with which to complete the ceremony. An order was accordingly given to the royal goldsmith, Sir Robert Vyner, to provide new regalia made after the old fashion, and some interesting particulars about these are to be found in the account of the coronation, by Sir Edward Walker, Garter Principal King of Arms, in a manuscript entitled *The Preparation for His Majesty's Coronation*, first published in 1820. Sir Robert Vyner's receipt for payment for these articles, dated 20th June 1662, still exists, and he acknowledges having received from the Royal Treasury £21,978, 9s. 11d., for—

 2 Crowns.
 2 Sceptres.
 A Globe of gold sett with diamonds, rubies, saphires, emeralds, and pearls.
 St. Edward's staffe.
 The Armilla.
 The Ampull.

But, altogether, Sir Robert Vyner's bill amounted to £32,000. Sir Edward Walker goes on to say :—

'Because through the Rapine of the late unhappy times, all the Royall Ornaments and Regalia heretofore preserved from age to age in the Treasury of the Church at Westminster, were taken away, sold and destroyed, the Comittee mett divers times not only to direct the remaking such Royall Ornaments and Regalia, but even to sette the form and fashion of each particular: all which doe now retayne the old names and fashion, although they have been newly made and prepared by orders given to the Earle of Sandwich, Master of the Great Wardrobe, and Sr Gilbert Talbott, Kn^t., Master of the Jewell House.

'Hereupon the Master of the Jewell House had order to provide two Imperial Crownes sett with pretious Stones, the one to be called St. Edward's Crowne, wherewith the king was to be crowned, and the other to be putt on after his Coronation, before his Maties retorne to Westminster Hall. Also

'An Orbe of Gold with a Crosse sett with pretious Stones.
'A Scepter with a Crosse sett with pretious Stones, called St. Edward's.
'A Scepter with a Dove sett with pretious Stones.
'A long Scepter, or Staffe of Gold with a Crosse upon the top, and a Pike at the foote of steele, called St. Edward's staffe.
'A Ring with a Ruby.
'A Paire of Gold Spurrs.
'A Chalice, and Paten of Gold.
'An Ampull for the Oyle and a spoone.
'And two Ingotts of Gold, the one a pound and the other a marke for the King's 2 Offerings.

'The master of the Great Wardrobe, had order also to provide the Ornaments to be called St. Edward's, wherein the King was to be crowned, viz. :—

THE ENGLISH REGALIA

'All these were laid ready upon the altar in the Quier.
> 'Colobium Sindonis, wch is of fine Linnen, of fashion of a Surplice with wide Sleeves. Supertunica, a Close Coate of Cloath of gold reaching to the heeles, lined with Crimosin Taffata, and guirt with a broad Girdle of Cloth of Gold to be putt over the Colobium.
> 'Armilla of the fashion of a stole made of Cloth of Gold to be putt about the neck, and fastned above and beneath the elbowes with silke Ribbands.
> 'A Pall of Cloth of Gold in the fashion of a cope.

'A Shirt of fine Linnen to be opened in the places for the anoynting. Over it another Shirt of red Sarcenet, and over that a Surcoat of Crimson Satten, which was made with a Collar for a Band, both opened for the anoynting, and closed with Ribbands.

'A paire of under Trowses, and Breeches over them, with Stockings fastened to the Trowses, all of Crimson Silke.

'layed on ye altar with the rest of the Ornaments.
> 'A paire of Hose or Buskins of Cloth of Gold.
> 'A paire of Sandalls of Cloth of Gold.

'A paire of Linnen Gloves.
'A linnen Coyfe.
'A Silke Towell to be held before the King at the Comunion, by the two Bishops.
'Three swords, vizt. Curtana, and two others, with Scabbards of Cloth of Gold.
'A Sword of State with a Rich Imbroydered Scabbard.'

The regalia and vestments as they now exist are certainly very near to the pattern of these just described. There are, fortunately, with Sir Edward Walker's manuscripts several drawings which, although they are somewhat elementary, are yet quite sufficient to show us that many of the designs then used, which were indeed themselves probably copies from some authority not now available, have been carefully preserved. The sceptre with the cross shows the upper part wreathed as it now is. The spurs, St. Edward's staff, and the sceptre with the dove, differ but slightly from those now in the Tower; the dove, however, is shown here, for the first time, standing upon a cross, and it is quite possible that all these items are now materially the same as when they were made by Sir Robert Vyner. The sword of state is quite different, as are the three other swords; and the top of 'Curtana,' the sword of mercy, is irregularly broken off instead of being smooth as now. The orb with the large amethyst under the cross, is probably the same as that now in the Tower with a few alterations; St. Edward's crown is the same in general design, but differs considerably in detail.

Most of our sovereigns have possessed second crowns, or crowns of state as they are called, and the designs of each of these have differed, although the same gems have been used over and over again in them. Unfortunately, in Sir Edward Walker's manuscript there are no figures given of the ampulla or the spoon.

THE ENGLISH REGALIA

The vestments are clearly figured: the supertunica, or dalmatic, has only a floral pattern upon it (fig. 1); the armilla, also, only has a floral pattern, but there is a cross patée at each end, and ribbons for tying it (fig. 2). The imperial mantle is embroidered with floral sprays arranged

FIG. 1.—THE SUPERTUNICA OR DALMATIC WORN BY CHARLES II. AT HIS CORONATION. FIG. 2.—THE ARMILLA OR STOLE WORN BY CHARLES II. AT HIS CORONATION.

in ovals, as in the existing mantle of Queen Victoria, and bears eagles, roses, fleurs-de-lys, and coronets (fig. 3).

Another valuable book concerning the coronation of Charles II., was written by John Ogilvy. It is called *The Entertainment of His Most Excellent Majestie Charles II. in his passage through the City of London to his Coronation*, etc. It was printed in London in 1662. The procession plates are by Wenceslaus Hollar, and they are very carefully and accurately drawn. The king is shown under the canopy, carried by the barons of the Cinque Ports, and he wears on his head only the royal cap of crimson velvet, turned up with miniver.

Among a collection of Exchequer records, which was discovered some time ago, was found an old bill dated 23rd February 1685. This bill was apparently made out to show the alterations necessary to be made in the existing regalia for the coronation of James II.

'A List of the Regalias provided for His late Majesty's coronation (Charles II.)

FIG. 3.—PALL OR ROYAL MANTLE WORN BY CHARLES II. AT HIS CORONATION.

FIG. 4.—THE PALL OR ROYAL MANTLE OF CLOTH OF GOLD WORN BY JAMES II. AT HIS CORONATION.

THE ENGLISH REGALIA

and are now in ye custody of Sr Gilbert Talbot, Knight, Master and Treasr of his Maty^s Jewells and plate, viz. :—

'Imprim. St. Edward's Crowne, poiz. 82 oz. 05 dwt. 16 gr.
    For ye addition of golde and workemanship, . . £350 0 0
    For ye loane of ye Jewells returned, . . . 500 0 0
'Item. One crowne of state, poiz. 72 oz. 01 dwt. 00 gr.
    For ye gold, Jewells and workemanship, . . . 7,870 0 0
'Item. One sceptre with a Dove, poiz. 34 oz. 03 dwt. 20 gr.
    For ye gold, Jewells and workemanship, . . . 440 0 0
'Item. One other sceptre with a cross, poiz. 32 oz. 11 dwt. 10 gr.
    For ye gold, Jewells and workemanship, . . . 1,025 0 0
'Itm. One St. Edward's staffe, poiz. 45 oz. 8 dwt. 8 gr.
    For ye gold and workemanship, . . . 225 6 2
'Itm. One Gloobe with a crosse, poiz. 49 oz. 7 dwt. 12 gr.
    For gold, Jewells and workemanship, . . . 1,150 0 0
'Itm. One pair of Spurrs, poiz. 12 oz. 18 dwt. 0 gr.
    For gold and workemanship, . . . 63 7 6
'Itm. Two armillas (bracelets), poiz. 6 oz. 12 dwt. 22 gr.
    For gold and workemanship, . . . 44 18 6
'Itm. One ampulla or Eglet, poiz. 21 oz. 8 dwt. 0 gr.
    For gold and workemanship, . . . 102 5 0
'Itm. The anointing spoon, poiz. 3 oz. 5 dwt. 0 gr.
    For silver and workemanship, . . . 2 0 0
'Itm. One chalice and paten, poiz. 61 oz. 12 dwt. 12 gr.
    For gold and workemanship, . . . 277 6 3
                                                        £12,050 3 5'

And there are other lists of things that have to be provided entirely anew. It is notable that the anointing spoon is again mentioned here as being made of silver.

The items of the regalia mentioned in this bill are illustrated in the *History of the Coronation of James II.*, written by his command by Francis Sandford, Lancaster Herald, and printed in the Savoy in 1687.

This admirable account of the coronation ceremonies contains two large plates of the regalia. On the first plate are figured the vestments. The imperial mantle has floral sprays arranged in ovals as already described, and also eagles, coronets, fleurs-de-lys and roses (fig 4). The supertunica of cloth of gold has still only floral sprays upon it (fig. 5). There is also a curious surcoat of crimson satin with openings left for the inunction (fig. 6). The armilla bears a rose as a centre ornament, and is further adorned with eagles, roses, coronets and fleurs-de-lys (fig. 7). There are detailed figures of the buskins, sandals and spurs, which are only in outline in Sir Edward Walker's account. The ampulla and the spoon are figured for the first time, and appear to be exactly the same as they are now. The coronation chair is also shown with designs upon it that certainly do not exist at the present day.

THE ENGLISH REGALIA

This chair, of course, is the one that all our kings have been crowned on at Westminster since Edward I. except Queen Mary I.; and, when Cromwell was installed Lord Protector, the chair was brought into Westminster Hall for him. The second plate contains figures of St. Edward's crown and the Queen's crown, a circlet worn by the Queen on her proceeding to her coronation, and two state crowns, to be worn

FIG. 5.—SUPERTUNICA OR DALMATIC WORN BY JAMES II. AT HIS CORONATION.

FIG. 6. SURCOAT OF CRIMSON SATIN—OPENED FOR THE ANOINTING ON BOTH SHOULDERS AND ON THE BEND OF THE ARMS AND AT THE BACK—WITH CRIMSON TAFFETA TIES. WORN BY JAMES II. AT HIS CORONATION.

by their Majesties after their coronation on their return to Westminster Hall—one for the King and one for the Queen.

St. Edward's crown shows substantially the same as it is now, but the setting of the gems is not quite so elaborate. The circlet worn by the Queen on her proceeding to her coronation, and her state crown, are both supposed to be now in the Tower, and are there described as having belonged to Queen Mary of Modena. But there are considerable differences between the figures and the actual crowns now existing; and it seems to me probable that both these crowns have been remade. Some of the gems from the King's state crown now find a place in Queen Victoria's, notably the large ruby forming the centre of the cross patée on the front of the crown. At the top of this crown was a cross patée

THE ENGLISH REGALIA

on a mound, the mound being 'one entire stone of a sea-water green known by the name of an agmarine.' This stone is cut in facets, and with the cross is still preserved in the Tower. The figure of the orb is nearly the same as it is now, 'on the top whereof is a very large amethist of a violet or purple colour encompassed with four silver wires.' St. Edward's staff is the same as now. The sceptre with the dove is probably the same as that now in the Tower. Then there are two sceptres with a cross: the first one, with the upper part wreathed, is probably that figured by Sir Edward Walker. The second sceptre with the cross appears for the first time; it was doubtless made for Queen Mary, and is now in the Tower with slight differences. The Queen's ivory rod, with a dove at the top, was also made for Queen Mary; and one of the larger plates, in the same book, shows King James and his Queen seated side by side, each crowned, and each holding two sceptres, one with a cross and one with a dove, so that with the exception of the holding of the orb, the Queen of James II. appears to have had equal ceremonial honour with his Majesty himself.

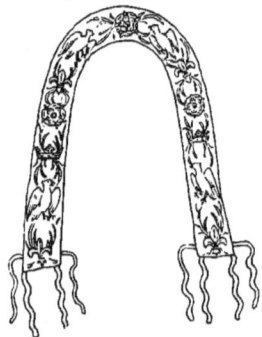

FIG. 7.—ARMILLA OR STOLE WORN BY JAMES II. AT HIS CORONATION.

Sandford also gives careful and valuable representations of the different parts of the coronation procession.

The coronation of William and Mary stands quite alone in the history of our coronations, as, during their reign as joint sovereigns, we possessed an actual King and an actual Queen. William declined to be Regent, and Mary refused to accept the crown, except with her husband, so it became in fact necessary that they should become joint sovereigns. This, of course, necessitated the making of a new orb, the smaller one now in the Tower. On their Great Seal they are represented as each having one hand upon a large orb; and in a print in the Bagford collection in the British Museum, dated 1689, and called the 'Protestants' Joy,' William and Mary are shown sitting under one canopy, each crowned and bearing a sceptre fleury in the right hand, and an orb with a cross in the left.

The next important book concerning the coronations of our kings was that issued under the authority, and by the care of, Sir George Nayler, Garter King of Arms, published in London in 1839, and illustrated magnificently by several artists—Stephanoff, and others. The book is an account of the coronation of George IV., July 19th 1821,

THE ENGLISH REGALIA

which was the most magnificent that has ever been held in England, the official cost of it having been £238,238. Some £5000 were allowed to Sir George Nayler by Government towards the cost of this splendid work, but even including this, as well as the fees paid by several peers for their portraits, the book is said to have been a financial failure. It not only shows the manner in which the various items of the regalia were carried in the procession, but the details of the official costume of the peers are so carefully reproduced that it may be fairly considered the best existing authority on that subject also. The Dean of Westminster is shown as carrying what is called the 'New Crown,' the setting of which is now the property of Lord Amherst of Hackney, and the cap still remaining within it is of blue velvet. As a general rule, the caps of English peers and sovereigns have been of crimson velvet, but in the case of this state crown of George IV., and presumably in one of Queen Elizabeth, the colour has been blue. I say presumably, because the only authority I have found for the blue cap in a crown of Queen Elizabeth's is a charming little book, bound in crimson velvet and adorned with enamels on gold, that was bound for her about 1570 and now forms part of the 'Old Royal' Library in the British Museum. In the centre of the upper side of this book there is a golden diamond-shaped plaque, on which is enamelled a red rose, ensigned with a royal crown having a blue cap. I do not say that this is an absolute authority, but in Queen Elizabeth's time the art of heraldry was much more exact than it is now, and it seems to me unlikely that so great a difference as that between blue and red would have been lightly made, especially on a book evidently intended for the Queen's own use.

VESTMENTS.

HE vestments that were used at the coronation of Queen Victoria are now in charge of an officer called the Keeper of the Robes, and are kept at St. James's Palace. They consist, like the vestments we have just been considering, of the

      Colobium Sindonis,
      Dalmatic,
      Stole,
      Imperial Mantle,

and to a considerable extent they preserve the ancient forms and designs of ornamentation.

  The Colobium Sindonis, the first vestment put upon the sovereign after the anointing, represents the alb of a priest, or the rochet of a bishop. It is a sleeveless garment of soft fine linen, edged with lace, and with a deep lace flounce of nine inches in depth (fig. 8). It is open at the side, and cut low at the neck, also edged all round with lace. It is gathered in at the waist and opens on the left shoulder, fastening with three small buttons. Upon the right shoulder are three sham buttons to match. At the coronation, a thick gold cord with heavy bullion tassels was worn at the waist over the 'colobium,' corresponding to the girdle of the alb.

  The Dalmatic, or supertunica, is put on after the Colobium Sindonis. It is a long jacket of cloth of gold, with wide pointed sleeves, without any fastening at all. The edges are all trimmed with gold lace. The design, woven into the cloth of gold, is a wavy pattern of palm leaves, outlined green, enclosing at regular intervals pink roses with green leaves, green shamrocks, and purple thistles. All these designs are in very pale colours, and the effect of them when the cloth of gold is moved is very delicate and beautiful. It is lined throughout with rose-coloured silk (fig. 9).

  The Stole now, in religious ceremonies, succeeds the alb immediately; but, in the coronation service, it succeeds the dalmatic, as it did in the eleventh and twelfth centuries, and it is so worn now by the Greek and Russian deacons. So here our kings preserve an ancient custom which the Western Church has lost. The stole was used at one time crossed over the breast, and one was found on the body of Edward I. worn in this manner, when his tomb at Westminster was opened in 1774; and it certainly was worn in this fashion abroad. This is the manner in which the stole is worn by a priest, but not by a bishop, when vested for mass. A fine example of this manner of wearing the royal stole can be seen on the beautiful golden bulla of the Emperor Frederick III., made in the fifteenth century. A specimen of it is now

THE ENGLISH REGALIA

exhibited in one of the show-cases in the British Museum. The Emperor holds a sceptre in his right hand and an orb in his left.

Queen Victoria's stole is a band of cloth of gold, three inches wide and five feet two inches long, with bullion fringe at each end. It is heavily embroidered with silver thread and a little colour. The centre ornament is a pink rose, the remaining ornaments are silver imperial eagles, silver and green shamrocks, silver, green, and purple thistles and

FIG. 8.—THE COLOBIUM SINDONIS WORN BY QUEEN VICTORIA AT HER CORONATION.   FIG. 9.—DALMATIC WORN BY QUEEN VICTORIA AT HER CORONATION.

pink roses. Each of these emblems is divided from the next one to it by a silver coronet, and at each end is a square panel with a blue and white torse above and below, worked with a red cross of St. George on a silver ground. It is lined with rose silk, and was worn by Queen Victoria hanging from the neck and depending at each side. It will be seen that the ornaments upon this stole resemble those of both Charles II. and James II., but that they are more ornate (fig. 10).

THE ENGLISH REGALIA

The Imperial Mantle is the last garment to be put upon the sovereign. The mediæval rubric describes this as four-square, embroidered with golden eagles. The four corners are supposed to represent the four quarters of the globe, subject to divine power, and it is analogous to the cope of a bishop. The magnificent mantle worn by Queen Victoria is sixty-five inches long, and measures across the shoulders twenty-eight inches. It is edged all round with golden bullion fringe two and a half inches deep, and is lined with rose-coloured silk. To the upper edge is attached a gold morse or clasp, with a silver edge faceted to represent diamonds (fig. 11). In the centre of this morse is the figure of an eagle in repoussé work, and at each of the sides a spray of rose, shamrock, and thistle similarly worked. There is a hook at the back of the neck to prevent the robe slipping. The design, woven into the cloth of gold, is a branched pattern arranged in ovals, outlined in purple silk and caught together by silver coronets and silver fleurs-de-lys alternately. In the spaces thus formed are red and white Tudor roses with green leaves, green shamrocks, purple and green thistles and silver eagles.

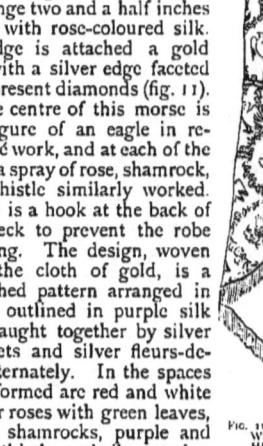

FIG. 10.—ARMILLA OR STOLE WORN BY QUEEN VICTORIA AT HER CORONATION.

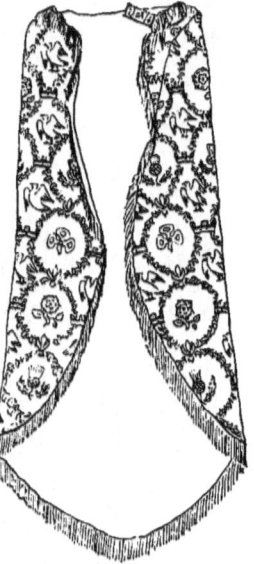

FIG. 11.—PALL OR IMPERIAL MANTLE WORN BY QUEEN VICTORIA AT HER CORONATION.

The coloured silks used in this mantle are in stronger tints than those used on the dalmatic. It will be observed that there is a strong similarity in the general design of the ornamentation of this garment and of that used on the mantles of Charles II. and James II.

ORBS.

THE orb with the cross above it is a very ancient Christian emblem. It was used by the Roman emperors, from whom it was borrowed by our Saxon kings. An instance of its early use exists in the British Museum on a magnificent carved ivory diptych of about the fifth century, representing an archangel holding in his left hand an orb with cross, very closely resembling that which is found on the Great Seal of Queen Elizabeth; in fact, we may say that the orb and the cross had been the emblem of independent Christian sovereignty longer than any other actual forms now used either here or on the Continent.

The orb is first found on English coins of Edward the Confessor,

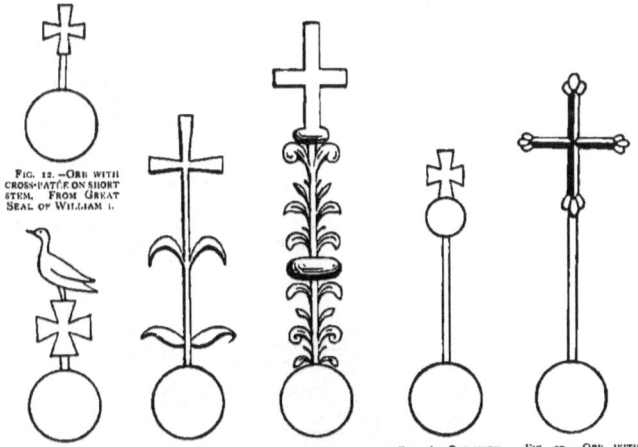

FIG. 12.—ORB WITH CROSS-PATÉE ON SHORT STEM. FROM GREAT SEAL OF WILLIAM I.

FIG. 13.—ORB WITH DOVE AND CROSS-PATÉE ON SHORT STEM. FROM THE FOURTH GREAT SEAL OF HENRY I.

FIG. 14.—ORB WITH CROSS ON TALL ORNAMENTAL STEM. FROM THE FIRST GREAT SEAL OF RICHARD I.

FIG. 15.—ORB WITH CROSS ON TALL ORNAMENTAL STEM. FROM THE FIRST GREAT SEAL OF HENRY III.

FIG. 16.—ORB WITH CROSS AND MOUND ON TALL STEM. FROM THE SECOND GREAT SEAL OF HENRY III.

FIG. 17.—ORB WITH ORNAMENTAL CROSS ON TALL STEM. FROM THE GREAT SEAL OF HENRY VII.

and shows as a sphere with a cross upon it. It does not occur often on coins, but may be seen upon some of those of the Tudor kings and the

THE ENGLISH REGALIA

finer coins of James I.; but on none of these is there any variation in its forms, and the cross is always a short one.

On the Great Seals of England, of which there is a complete series in the British Museum, there is a certain degree of difference in the forms of the orb. On the Great Seal of Edward the Confessor it first appears, and is a simple sphere held in his left hand. William I. used a cross above the sphere (fig. 12), and this cross in some form or other has invariably been used since. On Henry I.'s fourth Great Seal a dove is shown above the cross-patée (fig. 13), and Stephen and Henry II. used the same design. Richard I. (fig. 14) and John both used a tall, thin cross with leaves issuing from its stem; and Henry III. (fig. 15) carries a beautiful orb with a very tall ornamented stem bearing a cross above it, and on his second Great Seal an orb with a tall plain stem, and a smaller orb with cross-patée at the top (fig. 16). From Edward I. to Richard III. the stems of the crosses above the orb were very tall, and the crosses themselves small. Henry VII. carries an orb with a tall stem (fig. 17), above which is a much larger cross than was used by his immediate predecessors, and each of the ends of the cross are ornamented with a trefoil. Henry VII., on his second Seal, entirely does away with the stem on which the cross had hitherto been placed, and the cross, itself ornamented, rests directly on the top of the orb, as does that on the orb now in the Tower which was made for Mary II. The orb which was made by Sir Robert Vyner for Charles II., and which is now in the Tower, has a large amethyst beneath the cross, which may be considered to take the place of the stem upon which, as we have seen, the cross was superimposed from the time of William I. to Henry VIII. (fig. 18).

FIG. 18.—ORB WITH ORNAMENTAL CROSS, FROM SECOND GREAT SEAL OF HENRY VIII.

SCEPTRES.

N coins of earlier date than those of Æthelred II., there are no indications of sceptres carried by the kings; but on some of his coins occurs a rod with three pearls at the top (fig. 19). On some of the coins of Canute, this triple head develops into a clearly-marked trefoil (fig. 20). Although he retains the simpler form of the three pearls generally, Edward the Confessor shows sometimes a sceptre with a cross-patée at the top, the prototype of the present sceptre with the cross (fig. 21); and, on the reverse of his first Great Seal, he bears in his right hand a sceptre with a dove, the proto-

  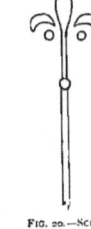  

FIG. 19.—SCEPTRE WITH THREE PEARLS AT THE TOP. FROM PENNY OF ÆTHELRED II.

FIG. 20.—SCEPTRE WITH TREFOIL AND PEARLS AT THE TOP. FROM PENNY OF CANUTE.

FIG. 21.—SCEPTRE WITH CROSS-PATÉE. FROM PENNY OF EDWARD THE CONFESSOR.

FIG. 22.—SCEPTRE WITH DOVE AT THE TOP. FROM FIRST GREAT SEAL OF EDWARD THE CONFESSOR.

type of the present sceptre with the dove (fig. 22). These two forms have subsisted from the time of Edward until to-day. Harold, on some of his coins, bears a sceptre with four pearls at the top (fig. 23), and further ornamentation on the handle. On some of the coins of William I. a distinct cross-patée is used, and William also uses a form of a triple leaf or flower, which is generally known as a sceptre-fleury; and one or other of these forms is found on coins until the time of John, after whose reign the sceptres seem to have been discontinued on coins until the time of Henry VII. Henry III., on his second Great Seal, bears a sceptre with a dove standing upon a small orb,—the first instance of this form (fig. 24).

On Edward III.'s second Seal 'of absence' he is shown holding a curious sceptre, the top of which is in the form of a small shrine or monstrance (fig. 25); and Henry IV., on his second Seal, shows a sceptre in which the top of the sceptre-fleury develops into a clearly-marked fleur-

THE ENGLISH REGALIA

de-lys (fig. 26); while Henry VI., on his Seal 'for French affairs,' carries a sceptre bearing at the top a 'hand of Justice.' This form is, however, a foreign one, and I do not think was ever used on a really English sceptre.

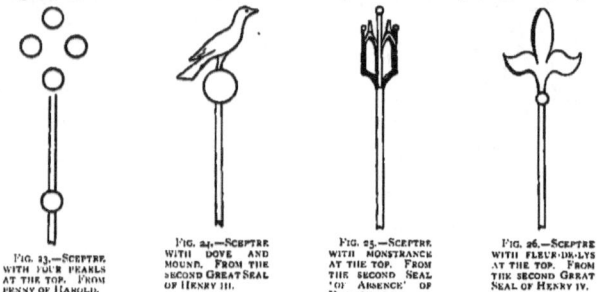

FIG. 23.—SCEPTRE WITH FOUR PEARLS AT THE TOP. FROM PENNY OF HAROLD.

FIG. 24.—SCEPTRE WITH DOVE AND MOUND. FROM THE SECOND GREAT SEAL OF HENRY III.

FIG. 25.—SCEPTRE WITH MONSTRANCE AT THE TOP. FROM THE SECOND SEAL 'OF ABSENCE' OF EDWARD III.

FIG. 26.—SCEPTRE WITH FLEUR-DE-LYS AT THE TOP. FROM THE SECOND GREAT SEAL OF HENRY IV.

On some of Henry VII.'s coins, and on others of a later date, the sceptre-fleury, more or less elaborate, constantly occurs, the only marked departure from this pattern being the ornamental emblematic sceptres found on the reverses of some of our gold coins, from the time of Charles II. until George I., the heads of which are in the forms of crosspatée, harp, thistle, and fleur-de-lys. These three latter are, however, evidently only symbolical, and are not likely to have had any real existence. Similar symbolical sceptres have occurred in recent times on some of our newer coinage, and on the reverse of some of our most recent issues occur typical representations of the sceptre with the orb and cross, and the sceptre with the dove. It will be noticed that the sceptres now existing in the Tower combine very completely the elements existing in the old forms of the sceptres of England as they are found on coins and Great Seals. The royal sceptre with the cross bears as its chief ornament the cross itself as used by Edward the Confessor; beneath this the sphere which first shows on the sceptre of Henry III., and the ornament that is now immediately under these is an elaborate modification of the arched crown.

The second, or Queen's, sceptre with the cross, has what may be called a double fleur-de-lys, which is in fact an amplification of the sceptre-fleury found on the coins of Canute. The sceptre with the dove is a very old form, and is not peculiar to England alone, as it has in fact a religious signification which is common to all Christian countries, and we in England inherit this form from Edward the Confessor, since whose time it has probably been used, by all our kings, whether it has been figured or not.

CROWNS.

ROWNS appear to have been at an early period worn by kings in battle, in order that they might be easily recognised; and, although it is quite possible that this outward sign of sovereignty may have marked the wearer as being entitled to special protection by his own men, it is also likely that it was often a dangerous sign of importance. Upon the authority of their coins, the heads of the early British kings were adorned with variously formed fillets and ornamental wreaths. Helmets are also evidently intended to be shown, and on some of the coins of Æthelstan the helmet bears upon it a crown of three raised points, with a single pearl at the top of each (fig. 27). Other coins bear the crown with the three raised points without the helmet (fig. 28). This crown of three points, bearing sometimes one and sometimes three pearls at the top of each, continued to be used by all the sole monarchs until Canute, on whose head a crown is shown, in which the three points develop into three clearly-marked trefoils (fig. 29).

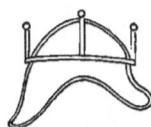 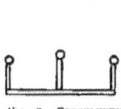 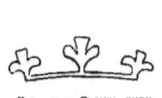 

FIG. 27.—CROWN, WITH THREE POINTS, BEARING EACH A SINGLE PEARL, ON HELMET. FROM PENNY OF ÆTHELSTAN.

FIG. 28.—CROWN WITH THREE POINTS, EACH BEARING ONE PEARL. FROM HALFPENNY OF ÆTHELSTAN.

FIG. 29.—CROWN WITH THREE TREFOILS. FROM PENNY OF CANUTE.

FIG. 30.—CROWN WITH ARCHES, PEARLS, AND PEARLED PENDANTS. FROM PENNY OF EDWARD THE CONFESSOR.

On the Great Seal of Edward the Confessor the king is wearing an ornamental cap, which is described by Mr. Wyon in his book about the Great Seals as bearing a crown with three points trefoiled; but the impressions of this Great Seal that I have been able to see are so indistinct in this particular, that I do not feel justified in corroborating his opinion. On some of the coins, however, of Edward the Confessor, an arched crown is very clearly shown, and this crown has depending from it, on each side, tassels with ornamental ends (fig. 30).

In the list of the English regalia which were destroyed under the Commonwealth in 1649 (see *ante*, p. 4) is found an item of great interest, viz. 'a gold wyer work crown with little bells,' which is there stated to have belonged to King Alfred, who appears to have been the first English king for whom the ceremony of coronation was used; and it is remarkable that on several of the crowns on coins and seals, from

THE ENGLISH REGALIA

the time of Edward the Confessor until Henry I., little tassels or tags are shown, which may indeed represent little bells suspended by a ribbon.

On King Alfred's own coins there is unfortunately nothing which can be recognised as a crown.

On the coins of Harold II. a crown is shown with arches, apparently intended to be jewelled, as is also the rim. There are also tassels with ornamental ends at the back of the crown (fig. 31).

William I., on his Great Seal, wears a crown with three points, at the top of each of which are three pearls (fig. 32), and on some of his coins a more ornamental form of crown occurs, having a broad jewelled rim and two arches, also apparently jewelled, and at each side are two pendants with pearl ends (fig. 33). William II. on his Great Seal has a crown

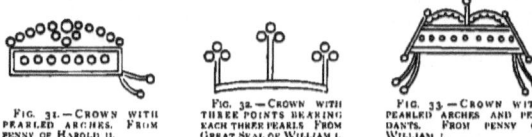

FIG. 31.—CROWN WITH PEARLED ARCHES. FROM PENNY OF HAROLD II.

FIG. 32.—CROWN WITH THREE POINTS BEARING EACH THREE PEARLS FROM GREAT SEAL OF WILLIAM I.

FIG. 33.—CROWN WITH PEARLED ARCHES AND PENDANTS. FROM PENNY OF WILLIAM I.

with five points (fig. 34), the centre one being slightly bigger than the others, and at the top of each a single pearl. At each side of the crown are pendants having three pearls at the ends.

On some of the coins of Stephen a pretty form of crown is seen. It has three fleurs-de-lys and two jewelled arches (fig. 35). The arches disappear from this time until the reign of Edward IV. On the Great Seal of Henry I. the king wears a simple crown with three fleur-de-lys points, and two pendants each with three pearls at the ends (fig. 36), and after this the pendants seem to have been discontinued.

FIG. 34.—CROWN WITH FIVE POINTS EACH BEARING ONE PEARL, WITH PEARLED PENDANTS. FROM GREAT SEAL OF WILLIAM II.

FIG. 35.—CROWN WITH THREE TREFOILS AND PEARLED ARCHES. FROM PENNY OF STEPHEN.

FIG. 36.—CROWN WITH THREE TREFOILS AND PEARLED PENDANTS. FROM GREAT SEAL OF HENRY I.

On the first Great Seal of Henry III. a crown with three fleurs-de-lys is shown surmounting a barred helmet (fig. 37), and Edward I. wore a similar crown with three fleurs-de-lys, but having supplementary pearls

THE ENGLISH REGALIA

between each (fig. 38); and this form lasted for a long time, as modifications of it are found on the coins of all the kings till Henry VII. On the third Great Seal of Edward IV. the king wears a crown with five fleurs-de-lys, the centre one being larger than the others, and the crown is arched and has at the top an orb and cross (fig. 39). Henry VI. on his first Seal

FIG. 37.—CROWN WITH THREE FLEURS-DE-LYS, ON HELMET. FROM FIRST GREAT SEAL OF HENRY I.

FIG. 38.—CROWN WITH THREE FLEURS-DE-LYS, AND PEARLS BETWEEN EACH. FROM PENNY OF EDWARD I.

FIG. 39.—CROWN WITH FIVE FLEURS-DE-LYS, AND ORNAMENTAL ARCHES WITH CROSS AT THE TOP. FROM THE THIRD GREAT SEAL OF EDWARD IV.

for foreign affairs, on which occurs the English shield, uses above it a crown with three crosses-patée and between each a pearl (fig. 40), this being the first distinct use of the cross-patée on the English crown, and it probably was used here in place of the fleur-de-lys hitherto worn in order to make a clear distinction between it and the French crown, which has the fleur-de-lys only and surmounts the coat of arms of that country. The king himself wears an arched crown, but the impressions are so bad that the details of it cannot be followed.

Henry VII. on his Great Seal uses, as ornaments for the crown, crosses-patée alternate with fleurs-de-lys, and also arches with an orb and cross at the top (fig. 41); and, on some of his coins, he reverts to the three fleurs-de-lys with points between them, arches being still used, with the orb and cross at the top (fig. 42). An ornamental form of crown bearing five ornamental leaves alternately large and small, with arches, orb, and cross at the top (fig. 43), occurs on the shillings of Henry VII.

FIG. 40.—CROWN WITH THREE CROSSES-PATÉE AND PEARLS BETWEEN THEM. FROM THE FIRST SEAL FOR FOREIGN AFFAIRS OF HENRY VI.

FIG. 41.—CROWN WITH CROSSES-PATÉE ALTERNATE WITH FLEURS-DE-LYS, WITH ARCHED MOUND AND CROSS AT THE TOP. FROM GREAT SEAL OF HENRY VII.

FIG. 42.—CROWN WITH THREE FLEURS-DE-LYS, AND TALL POINTS BETWEEN THEM, WITH MOUND AND CROSS AT THE TOP. FROM GROAT OF HENRY VII.

FIG. 43.—CROWN WITH FIVE ORNAMENTED TREFOILS, ARCHED, WITH MOUND AND CROSS AT THE TOP. FROM SHILLING OF HENRY VII.

On the crowns of Henry VIII. as well as upon his Great Seals, the alternate crosses-patée and fleurs-de-lys are found on the rim of the

THE ENGLISH REGALIA

crown, which is arched, and has an orb and cross at the top, and this is the form that has remained ever since (fig. 44). So we may consider that the growth of the ornament on the rim of the crown has followed a regular sequence from the points with one pearl at the top, of Æthelstan, to the trefoil of Canute; the arches began with Edward the Confessor, and the centre trefoil turned into the cross-patée of Henry VI. The fact that the remaining trefoils turned eventually into fleurs-de-lys is only, I think, a natural expansion of form, and does not appear to have had anything to do with the French fleur-de-lys, which was adopted as an heraldic bearing for an entirely different reason. The royal coat of arms of England did bear for a long time in one of its quarterings the actual fleurs-de-lys of France, and this, no doubt, has given some reason to the idea that the fleurs-de-lys on the crown had also something to do with France; but, as a matter of fact, they had existed on the crown of England long anterior to our use of them on the coat of arms, as well as remaining there subsequently to their discontinuance on our royal escutcheon.

FIG. 44.—CROWN WITH CROSSES-PATÉE AND FLEURS-DE-LYS ALTERNATE, ARCHED, WITH MOUND AND CROSS AT THE TOP. FROM CROWN OF HENRY VIII.

The cross-patée itself may possibly have been evolved in a somewhat similar way from the three pearls of William I., as we often find the centre trefoil, into which, as we have seen, these three points eventually turned, has a tendency to become larger than the others; and this difference has been easily made more apparent by squaring the ends of the triple leaf. At the same time, it must not be forgotten that the cross-patée was actually used on the sceptre of Edward the Confessor, so it is just possible it may have had some specially English significance.

I have already mentioned that as well as the official crown of England, which alone I have just been describing, there has often been a second or state crown, and this, although it has in general design followed the pattern of the official crown, has been much more elaborately ornamented, and in it has been set and reset the few historic gems possessed by our nation. The fact that these state crowns have in turn been denuded of their jewels, accounts for the fact that the old settings of some of them still exist.

Charles II.'s state crown is figured in Sir Edward Walker's account of his coronation, but the illustration of it is of such an elementary character that little reliance can be placed on it; the actual setting of this crown, however—which was the one stolen by Colonel Blood on May 13th, 1671—is now the property of Lord Amherst of Hackney, and the spaces from which the great ruby and the large sapphire—both of which are now in Queen Victoria's state crown—have been taken, are clearly seen (fig. 45). James II.'s state crown, which is very accurately figured in Sandford's account of his coronation, and pieces of which are still in

THE ENGLISH REGALIA

the Tower, also had this great ruby as its centre ornament (fig. 46). In Sir George Nayler's account of the coronation of George IV., there is a figure of his so-called 'New Crown,' the arches of which are composed of oak-leaf sprays with acorns, and the rim adorned with laurel sprays (fig. 47). The setting of this crown also belongs to Lord Amherst of Hackney, and so does another setting of a small state queen's crown, the ownership of which is doubtful. William IV. appears to have had a very beautiful state crown, with arches of laurel sprays and a cross at the top with large diamonds. It is figured in Robson's *British Herald*, published in 1830 (fig. 48).

FIG. 45.—THE STATE CROWN OF CHARLES II.   FIG. 46.—THE STATE CROWN OF JAMES II.   FIG. 47.—THE STATE CROWN OF GEORGE IV.   FIG. 48.—THE STATE CROWN OF WILLIAM IV.

There is one other crown of great interest which, since the time of James Sixth of Scotland and First of England, forms part of our regalia. This is the crown of Scotland, and is the most ancient piece of state jewellery of which we can boast.

Edward I. after his defeat of John Baliol in 1296, carried off the crown of Scotland to England, and Robert Bruce had another made for himself. This in its turn, after Bruce's defeat at Methven, fell into Edward's hands. Another crown seems to have been made for Bruce in 1314, when he was established in the sovereignty of Scotland after Bannockburn, and the present crown probably consists largely of the material of the old one, and most likely follows its general design. It has, however, much French work about it, as well as the rougher gold work made by Scottish jewellers, and it seems probable that the crown, as it now is, is a reconstruction by French workmen made under the care and by the order of James V. about 1540. It was with this crown that Queen Mary was crowned when she was nine months old.

In 1661 the Scottish regalia were considered to be in danger from the English, and were sent to Dunnottar Castle for safety. From 1707 until 1818 they were locked up in a strong chest in the Crown-room of Edinburgh Castle, and Sir Walter Scott, in whose presence the box was opened, wrote an account of them in 1819. The crown consists of a fillet of gold bordered with flat wire. Upon it are twenty-two large stones,

THE ENGLISH REGALIA

set at equal distances—*i.e.* nine carbuncles, four jacynths, four amethysts, two white topazes, two crystals with green foil behind them, and one topaz with yellow foil. Behind each of these gems is a gold plate, with bands above and below of white enamel with black spots, and between each stone is a pearl. Above the band are ten jewelled rosettes, and ten fleurs-de-lys alternately, and between each a pearl. Under the rosettes and fleurs-de-lys are jewels of blue enamel and pearls alternately. The arches have enamelled leaves of French work in red and gold upon them, and the mount at the top is of blue enamel, studded with gold stars. The cross at the top is black enamel, with gold arabesque patterns; in the centre is an amethyst, and in this cross and in the corners are Oriental pearls set in gold. At the back of the cross are the letters I. R. V. in enamel work. On the velvet cap are four large pearls, in settings of gold and enamel (fig. 49).

FIG. 49.—THE SCOTTISH CROWN.

Generally, the Scottish work in gold is cast solid and chased, the foreign work being thinner and repoussé. Several of the diamonds are undoubtedly old, and are cut in the ancient Oriental fashion, and many of the pearls are Scottish. It is kept in Edinburgh Castle with the rest of the Scottish regalia. None of the other pieces at all equal it in interest, as with the exception of the coronation ring of Charles I. they are of foreign workmanship, or, at all events, have been so altered that there is little or no original work left upon them.

The coronation ring just mentioned is, however, worthy of special remark, these rings having been usually kept as the personal property of the sovereigns for whom they were made. It consists of a pale ruby with red foil behind it, engraved on which is a couped cross, enclosed in a circle of twenty-six table diamonds, set close and foiled at the back. It formed part of the bequest of Cardinal York to George III., and is very interesting because, although a ring has formed part of the coronation jewels from the earliest times, this is the only existing one which is the property of the nation. It was, moreover, evidently intended originally to be used by different people, as it is jointed like a bracelet with a very long spring to the snap, and is capable of fitting fingers of different sizes (fig. 50).

FIG. 50.—THE CORONATION RING OF CHARLES I.

Although it is not now part of the royal treasure, there is one remarkable piece of plate existing which ought to be so: and a note concerning it may perhaps not be out of place here, as it may to some extent serve to show what magnificent works of art our sovereigns once possessed. It is a splendid enamelled gold cup of the fourteenth century which belonged to our kings from the time of Henry VI. until James I.,

THE ENGLISH REGALIA

who gave it away. But if it is not now among the regalia it is next thing to it, as it is the property of the nation, and forms one of the chief ornaments of the wonderful 'gold room' at the British Museum. It is certainly one of the finest specimens of mediæval enamel work existing. The cup originally was on a short stem, but under the Tudors it was heightened, and the added piece bears characteristic Tudor enamels in high relief. On the cup itself, the lid and the foot, are shown in lustrous translucent enamel events in the life of St. Agnes; round the edges of the foot and the lid were ornamental edgings of gold and pearls, much of which is now gone; and the actual top, which no doubt was very ornamental, is also gone.

The history of this cup has been carefully traced, and it formed part of the treasure of France as well as England; its actual beginning is, however, still in mystery.

THE AMPULLA.

R. CHAFFERS, in his book on English goldsmiths, says: 'The ancient ampulla, used at the coronation of English sovereigns, was, according to Mezeray, of lapis lazule, with a golden eagle at the top enriched with pearls and diamonds.' Of course there is no relic of this beautiful jewel left, neither is there any indication of the size given; but the mention of a golden eagle is interesting, as it at all events shows, that if we have kept nothing else, we have kept the tradition.

There is an ancient legend that a holy cream was given to St. Thomas of Canterbury, by the Virgin Mary, for the anointing of the kings of England. This cream was preserved in a golden eagle, which was also divine. The only Christian kings which used to be anointed were the kings of England, France, Jerusalem, and Sicily, and afterwards the kings of Scotland, by special Papal favour. The kings of England and France had a special additional right to be anointed with the holy cream or chrisma—a sacred unguent made chiefly of olive oil and balm, and only used in the more sacred ceremonies of the Church, ordination of priests, consecration of bishops, and a few other functions, in all of which it was considered to confer a specially sacred character to persons to whom it was given. Elaborate directions are given, in coronation services, for the royal anointing. This usually includes the making of a cross on the king's head with the chrisma; on the other places, the hands, the breast, the shoulders, etc., the anointing was done with holy oil. James II. paid his apothecary, 'James St. Armand, Esq.,' £200 for the cream for his coronation.

The golden eagle itself measures about nine inches in height, with the pedestal. The diameter of the pedestal is three and a half inches. The stretch of the wings is seven inches. It weighs about ten ounces of solid gold, and the cavity of the body is capable of containing about six ounces of oil. The head screws off at the neck for the cavity to be filled, and the oil pours out at the beak. This pouring out of the oil, as well as dipping the fingers in the spoon and anointing the sovereign, is always done by the Archbishop of Canterbury.

Mr. W. Jones, in his book on *Crowns and Coronations*, published in London in 1883, says: 'It is said that the eagle now existing is the real original ampulla, which was first used at the coronation of Henry IV.' (Oct. 13th 1399). Few of those that have written about this eagle venture to give any opinion about its antiquity, and, at first sight, it certainly does not seem very old on the surface. The pedestal is, I think, clearly

THE AMPULLA.

of seventeenth century make, and the whole of the bird, down to the minutest feathers, has been gone over with chased work, probably at the same period; but I think it will be admitted that the general form of the bird lends probability to the theory that it was made at a much earlier time, especially the body (fig. 51). Undoubtedly there is one thing about it that is much earlier than Charles II., and that is the very primitive screw with which the head screws on. So that, at all events, it seems to me very probable that Sir Robert Vyner found the body of an ancient eagle at Westminster when he had to remake the regalia for Charles II., and that he added a pedestal and wings to this body, and went over the whole surface with a graver. The eagle itself is an emblem of imperial domination. It may be an indication of the ancient claim of the sovereigns of England to be Emperors of Britain and Lords Paramount of all the islands of the West.

Fig. 51.—The Ampulla.

Sandford gives an engraving of the ampulla, which appears exactly as it is to-day. He considered it to be an ancient piece of plate, and says that this and the spoon were preserved from destruction by having been kept at Westminster.

THE SPOON.

TWO of the articles now existing among the regalia kept in the Tower are possibly, at least in part, of great age. These are the golden ampulla, or eagle, for holding the anointing oil, and the anointing spoon. Both of these have marks upon them of considerable antiquity, and of the two the spoon has been less altered than the eagle. Before describing the spoon as I see it, it will be as well to note what antiquaries of authority have already said concerning it.

Henry Shaw, in his exquisitely illustrated book on the dresses and decorations of the Middle Ages, published in London in 1843, gives a fine coloured illustration of the spoon. He says, 'It has most probably been used in the coronation of our monarchs since the twelfth century,' . . . 'its style of ornamentation seems to prove that it was made at that period,' . . . 'there can of course be no doubt of its antiquity.' He says it is of gold—a natural mistake; but as a matter of fact it is of silver, heavily gilt. He restores the handle itself with blue enamel, and the two circles above and below the pearls with green enamel.

Mr. William Chaffers, in his book on English goldsmiths, arguing from Sir Robert Vyner's inventory of the new regalia in 1684, says it is 'evident that the coronation spoon was actually made at this time.' He further professes to see interlaced C's in the ornamentation of the bowl, and considers Shaw was mistaken in his description.

Mr. W. Jones, in his book on *Crowns and Coronations*, published in London in 1883, says: 'The spoon from its extreme thinness appears to be ancient'; and 'it seems probable that this spoon may have been used at the coronation of our monarchs since the twelfth century.'

Mr. Cripps, in *Old English Plate*, considers the entry in the lists of the regalia in the time of Charles II. to prove that the coronation spoon was at all events remade for him. Lastly, in 1890, when a most valuable paper on *The Spoon and its History* was read at the Society of Antiquaries by Mr. C. J. Jackson, F.S.A., and her Majesty was graciously pleased to lend this specimen for exhibition, the general opinion was that it might be attributed to the twelfth or thirteenth centuries.

I have myself examined the spoon very carefully, and have come to the conclusion that the handle at all events is undoubtedly old. This part of the spoon is about seven and a half inches long. It is divided into three parts, and tapers towards the end. The end division is wreathed, and the extreme tip is of a flattened cup-like form. Then comes a boss which may represent a grotesque animal's head. Next is a

THE CORONATION SPOON.
FRONT VIEW.

QUEEN ELIZABETH'S
SALT-CELLAR.

THE CORONATION SPOON.
SIDE VIEW.

THE ENGLISH REGALIA

division that at one time contained enamel; the metal-work on this is not filagree, as described by Mr. Shaw, but 'champlevé,' an older form of preparation for enamel-work. The lower surface is rough, as might be expected, but no traces now remain of enamel. The pattern is a decorated scroll. Then comes a square boss with rounded corners, having a chased circle on each of its faces, which marks the beginning of the third and most decorative part of the handle, which thickens considerably in the centre. A circular ornament, with traces of chased work upon it, is the chief attempt at decoration. Above and below this are two pearls, and beyond these two circular ornamental spaces with 'champlevé' work, which Mr. Shaw shows filled with green enamel. Then next to the spoon is an ornament which somewhat resembles a fanciful head, and the stem is joined to the bowl by a prolongation downwards, a modification of the 'keel and disc' fashion well known to have been used in early Christian spoons. This handle shows to my eyes no sign whatever of recent workmanship, either on the sides, the front, or the back. The patterns on the back are quite simple, and the knot in the thickest part is certainly of an ancient design. All the corners are rounded everywhere, and the forms show wear consistently all over it; but it looks new at first sight in consequence of having recently been heavily gilded. The regilding may have destroyed small bits of enamel which in Shaw's time may have existed in protected corners, and given him some authority for his green and blue restorations.

The bowl, which is about two and a quarter inches long, has work upon it which is more difficult to fix as having been made at any particular time. In the first place, the shape of it does not agree with the generally understood shapes used in mediæval domestic spoons. It is divided by a ridge down the middle into two parts, into which the Archbishop dips his two fingers, and at its junction with the stem there is an engraved leaf pattern the treatment of which is comparatively modern. The front of the bowl is engraved with a design which has some appearance of antiquity, but the manner of treating it does not appear altogether satisfactory. Indeed it appears to me very probable that the bowl was remade by Sir Robert Vyner, and that the ancient bowl may have had the curious ridge down the middle, although I hardly think it had the pattern on the front or the leaf pattern at the back.

In the various entries in which a spoon is mentioned it will be noticed that the sums set down for the work are small; and even in the seventeenth century, the date of these lists, it would hardly have been sufficient to pay for such a work of art.

It is also noteworthy that in the various accounts where a spoon is mentioned nothing is said about the enamelling, which undoubtedly existed, neither is there any mention of the four pearls. For these

THE ENGLISH REGALIA

reasons I am inclined to think some other spoon must have been made of a cheaper kind, this one having been for the time mislaid, or hidden for safety somewhere at Westminster.

Both this spoon and the golden eagle have some sort of sacredness connected with them. They are both used in that part of the coronation which is specially holy, and when the regalia were removed to the Tower from Westminster Abbey it is quite possible to imagine that these two precious objects were retained by the Abbey authorities on the ground of their belonging to them; indeed, Sandford, speaking of the plunder of the regalia from Westminster Abbey, expressly excepts the ampul and spoon, and it is therefore reasonable to believe that these were kept separately. He says: 'All the regalia *except the ampul and spoon* (all which were constantly kept in the church of Westminster) being sacrilegiously plundered away.'

QUEEN ELIZABETH'S SALT-CELLAR.

AMONG the many lists of royal treasure in Rymer's *Fœdera* is one which gives details of the plate which was given to the Duke of Buckingham and the Earl of Holland to sell for Charles I. in 1625 on the occasion of his trouble with Spain. Unfortunately no figures are given, but the descriptions are elaborate enough to show that many of the pieces must have been of great beauty. There are also minute descriptions of many of these treasures given in the Calendars of the Exchequer from Edward II. to Henry VIII. What with one king selling some, and another king losing some, and the Commonwealth making at last a clean sweep of anything royal they could lay hands upon, it is little wonder that there are but few pieces left of the old royal treasure of England. Among the fine collection at the Tower is only one piece that can claim any greater age than the time of Charles II., and this is known as Queen Elizabeth's 'Great' Salt-cellar. Salt-cellars, it should be said, were called 'Great' in distinction from the 'Trencher' salts, being used to mark the difference in rank between the

THE ENGLISH REGALIA

guests at table, whereas the latter, which were quite small, were put near each guest for use only.

This salt-cellar is in three divisions—the lower part, which holds the salt in a shallow basin, then four brackets, and the lid raised upon them.

This arrangement is peculiar, and it seems as if the lid was at one time fitted in the lower portion, and that it had been lifted up on the brackets by way of improvement. The brackets as they now are do not appear to be of the same workmanship, or to be quite in keeping with the rest, but they may have been substituted for others which originally existed in the same place, or made to match others of Charles II.'s which have the same kind of heightening.

The body of the salt-cellar is divided externally into three compartments by grotesque figures with scroll prolongations and flat pieces curving outwards above their heads, terminating in masks.

In each compartment is an allegorical figure of one of the Virtues within a circular wreath, charmingly designed and executed in low repoussé and fine chased work. The foot has two decorated bands: one flat with an elaborate design of cupids and flowers, and the lower one curved outwards and covered with masks, flat scrolls, and conventional flower sprays. There are three feet designed in the form of sphinxes' heads with forepaws.

Above the allegorical figures the lip broadens out into a projecting piece ornamented with fruits and flowers in high relief, and over this is the shallow salt basin.

The four scrolls supporting the top are in the form of dolphins with ornamental tails, and the lid itself is a very fine specimen of Elizabethan goldsmith's work. The main part of the lid is ornamented with fruit and flower groups and characteristic strap and cartouche work, and allegorical figures within oval laurel wreaths. Above this comes an urn-like superstructure with three scroll handles having animals' feet and human masks. A smaller urn form supports the figure of a knight in armour with a long sword and a shield.

ST. EDWARD'S CROWN.

ST. EDWARD'S Crown was made for the coronation of Charles II. in 1662, by Sir Robert Vyner. It was ordered to be made as nearly as possible after the old pattern, and the designs of it that have been already mentioned as existing in the works of Sir Edward Walker, and Francis Sandford, show that in essential form it was the same as now; indeed, the existing crown is in all probability mainly composed of the same materials as that made by Sir Robert. The crown consists of a rim or circlet of gold, adorned with rosettes of precious stones, surrounded by diamonds, and set upon enamel arabesques of white and red. The centre gems of these rosettes are rubies, emeralds, and sapphires. Rows of large pearls mark the upper and lower edges of the rim, from which rise four crosses-patée, and four fleurs-de-lys alternately, adorned with diamonds and other gems. The gem clusters upon the crosses are set upon enamel arabesques of white and red, of similar workmanship to that upon the rim. From the tops of the crosses rise two complete arches of gold, crossing each other, and curving deeply downwards at the point of intersection. These arches are considered to be the mark of independent sovereignty. They are edged with rows of large pearls, and have gems and clusters of gems upon them, set on arabesques of red and white, like those upon the crosses. From the intersection of the arches springs a mound of gold, encircled by a fillet from which rises a single arch, both of which are ornamented with pearls and gems. On the top of the arch is a cross-patée of gold, set in which are coloured gems and diamonds. At the top of the cross is a large spheroidal pearl, and from each of the side arms, depending from a little gold bracket, is a beautifully formed pear-shaped pearl. The crown is shown in the Tower, with the crimson velvet cap, turned up with miniver, which would be worn with it.

This crown is very large, but whether it is actually worn or not it would always be present at the coronation, as it is the 'official' crown of England.

ST. EDWARD'S CROWN.

THE ROYAL SCEPTRE WITH THE CROSS.

THE Royal Sceptre with the Cross is of gold, and is figured in Sir Edward Walker's account of the coronation of Charles II. (fig. 52); it is also shown in the same form, namely a fleur-de-lys with orb and cross, but a little more elaborate, in Sandford (fig. 53), and also in the account of the coronation of George IV. by Sir George Nayler.

The mound at the top is not specially described by Sir Edward Walker, but Sandford describes it as an amethyst, and in George the Fourth's Coronation Book it is shown blue, which doubtless indicates the same stone. The fleur-de-lys, which formerly supported this mound, has now disappeared, and is replaced by an elaborate piece of goldsmith's work, in general form resembling an arched crown thickly jewelled with coloured gems and diamonds, with supplementary curves and sprays of beautiful enamels. On this glittering foot the great amethyst orb rests, supported by jewelled projections rising upwards. It is faceted all over, and round the centre is a jewelled band with arch of gold and diamonds. The cross-patée at the top is thickly set with diamonds, an especially large one being in the middle. The head of this sceptre is so glittering and brilliant that it is difficult to make out the details of its form except by a very close examination, and it is indeed a marvellous and beautiful piece of jewellery. The entire length of the sceptre is two feet nine and a quarter inches, and the upper part is wreathed, collars of gems and enamels enclose a smooth portion as a grip, and the end is encrusted with rich sprays of gold and enamels thickly jewelled with coloured stones and diamonds. The foot widens out into an orb or boss with ornamental gold work upon it, and it is possible that all of the sceptre except the part immediately below the mound is the same as was originally made by Sir Robert Vyner, although it is likely that it has been repaired and that the enamels have been remade since his time.

FIG. 52.—THE ROYAL SCEPTRE WITH THE CROSS. FROM SIR EDWARD WALKER'S ACCOUNT OF THE CORONATION OF CHARLES II.

FIG. 53.—THE ROYAL SCEPTRE WITH CROSS, MOUND AND FLEUR-DE-LYS, USED FROM JAMES II. TO GEORGE IV. INCLUSIVE. FROM SANDFORD'S ACCOUNT OF THE CORONATION OF JAMES II.

This sceptre is placed in the right hand of the sovereign at the coronation.

THE QUEEN'S SCEPTRE WITH THE CROSS.

HE Queen's Sceptre with the Cross is first figured in Sandford, as it was made for Queen Mary of Modena (fig. 54); and with trifling alterations, that now existing in the Tower agrees with his account.

The sceptre is all of gold ornamented with diamonds. At the top is a double fleur-de-lys, with three leaves bending upwards and three bending downwards, all thickly jewelled with diamonds of fair size. Above this is a mound of gold with a fillet set thickly with diamonds, and an arch over the top of the globe jewelled in the same way. The cross-patée at the top has a large diamond in each of its arms and a large one in the centre. In the middle of the sceptre is a space closely ornamented with sprays formed of open work in gold, with leaves and flowers composed of large and small diamonds. Beyond this is a clear space and an elaborately jewelled boss at the end. It is two feet ten inches in length.

FIG. 54.—SCEPTRE WITH CROSS, MOUND AND FLEUR-DE-LYS, MADE FOR MARY OF MODENA, QUEEN-CONSORT OF JAMES II.

THE LARGER ORB.

THE ROYAL SCEPTRE
WITH THE CROSS.

THE QUEEN'S SCEPTRE
WITH THE CROSS.

THE LARGER ORB.

HE orb, mound, or globe is placed in the sovereign's right hand on being crowned, and after that is carried in the left hand (fig. 55). It was used by the early Christians, and was borrowed from the Roman Emperors by our Saxon kings; it is never put into the hands of any but kings or queens regnant. The orb of England is remarkable for the fine amethyst cut in facets, one and a half inches in height, on which the cross-patée stands. The golden ball itself is six inches in diameter, and has a fillet of gold round the centre, outlined by fine pearls and ornamented with clusters of gems, set in borders of white and red enamel of similar workmanship to that upon St. Edward's crown. The centre stones of these clusters are large rubies, sapphires, and emeralds alternately, and in each case the coloured stones are surrounded by diamonds. An arch of similar design to the fillet crosses the upper part of the orb, and the beautiful cross above the large amethyst has in the centre on one side an emerald, and on the other a sapphire. The outlines of the cross are marked by rows of diamonds, and there are three large diamonds down the centre of each arm. The jewels in the centre of each side are also encircled by diamonds, and between the lower foot of the cross and the amethyst is a collar of small diamonds. At the end of each of the upper arms of the cross is a large pearl, and in each of the four inner corners is also a large pearl.

hIC DEDERVNT: hAROLDO CORONA REGIS

FIG. 55.—THE CORONATION OF HAROLD II. FROM THE BAYEUX TAPESTRY. THE KING IS CROWNED, AND CARRIES AN ORB IN HIS LEFT HAND AND A SCEPTRE IN HIS RIGHT.

This orb was made by Sir Robert Vyner for Charles II. It is figured in Sir Edward Walker's account of his coronation. The large amethyst is clearly shown, but the bands encircling it are of a different and more ornate pattern from those now existing. It is thus certain that something has been done to the orb since it was first made, but probably the extent of this alteration has been a re-setting of gems and the re-making of all the enamel-work.

THE SCEPTRE WITH THE DOVE.

THE Sceptre with the Dove is of gold, and both in Walker's account of the coronation of Charles II. and Sandford's of that of James II. (fig. 56) it is shown as bearing the same general design as that now existing. It is a rod of gold measuring three feet seven inches in length. At the top is a mound, also of gold, with a fillet round the centre, studded with diamonds, and an arch above it, ornamented in the same way. From the top of the mound rises a golden cross, on which is sitting a dove, with extended wings, of white enamel; the eye, beak, and feet are of gold. A little below the mound is a band studded with diamonds, and beneath this another band, with drooping designs, ornamented with coloured gems and diamonds. In the centre of the sceptre is an ornament of enamels and gems, and gold open work with coloured gems and diamonds. Nearer to the end is another band with large jewels, and at the foot is a boss encircled with a jewelled band and also an enamelled band. The dove is typical of the Holy Ghost, who was considered especially to control the actions of kings, and for this reason the sceptre with the dove has been constantly used by kings from a very remote period. In France it was formerly the custom to let white doves loose in the church, after the coronation of the kings.

FIG. 56.—SCEPTRE WITH DOVE, CROSS AND MOUND. FROM SIR EDWARD WALKER'S ACCOUNT OF THE CORONATION OF CHARLES II.

This sceptre is borne in the left hand of the sovereign at the coronation.

THE SMALLER ORB.

THE QUEEN'S SCEPTRE
WITH THE DOVE.

THE QUEEN'S SCEPTRE WITH THE DOVE.

HE Second, or Queen's, Sceptre with the Dove resembles the King's, but is a little smaller.

The mound at the top is surmounted by a cross on which is a white enamelled dove with outstretched wings. Encircling the mound is a fillet ornamented with coloured gems and diamonds and leaves enamelled white and red. The arch over the top of the mound is decorated in a similar manner. About the middle of the sceptre is a collar of dark blue enamel ornamented with gems and designs in white enamel. Nearer to the foot is another more elaborate collar with sprays of open work in gold ornamented thickly with gems and enamels. The foot of the sceptre is a boss with ornaments of gold gems and enamels.

This sceptre is not mentioned in Sandford's account of the coronation of James II. The Queen on that occasion used only the small ivory sceptre with the dove with closed wings.

This small ivory sceptre would very probably not have been considered near enough in design to the King's to satisfy the desire for equality of ceremony which was so prevalent at the coronations of William and Mary. So it is nearly certain that this larger gold sceptre with the dove was made for Mary II., and that it was purposely made very like the King's. It was lost for some time, owing probably to some of the many changes that have at various times taken place in the Tower, but was discovered in 1814 at the back of a shelf in the Jewel-house.

THE SMALLER ORB.

S I have shown before, there was some trouble about the coronation of William and Mary, and in some instances the regalia had to be doubled. No doubt what could be altered was altered, so that many of the things which were only intended for the use of a Queen-consort actually did duty for a Queen-regnant; but one thing had to be made entirely anew, and that was an orb, so that the Queen as well as her husband should have the necessary emblem of independent sovereignty. But the orb which was made for her is by no means so handsome as the older one. It is not quite so large. It has a fillet round the centre outlined with large pearls, and ornamented with rubies, sapphires, and emeralds, alternately circular and octagonal, set in collars of gold. An arch crosses the upper half, ornamented in a similar manner, and at the top a cross-patée rests immediately on the orb, and is studded with rubies, sapphires, and diamonds, differently arranged on each side.

ST. EDWARD'S STAFF.

SO many of the pieces of our regalia are called after Saint Edward the Confessor, that he may indeed almost be called the patron saint of the regalia. Henry III. rebuilt Westminster Abbey in his honour, and he is godfather not only to our official English crown, but to the sword 'Curtana,' and the curious rod of justice and equity. A rod of this kind has been used at all our coronations from the earliest times. The one now extant seems to be the only article among the regalia which is the same now in every respect as it was originally when made by Sir Robert Vyner. It is supposed to be a staff to guide the footsteps of the king. It is tipped with a pike or foot of steel four inches and a quarter in length.

The entire length of St. Edward's staff is four feet seven inches and a half, and it is a rod of gold divided at intervals with collars of ornamental leaf patterns. At the top is a mound and cross-patée, and tradition says that formerly a piece of the true Cross was enclosed within the mound.

THE QUEEN'S IVORY ROD.

IN the list of the regalia destroyed under the Commonwealth in 1649 an entry will be found of an ivory staff with a dove at the top, and such a staff is now in the Tower. It is there stated to have been made for Mary of Modena, Queen-consort of James II., and is very likely to be a copy of the older sceptre. It is made in three pieces with collars of gold over the junctions, and measures altogether three feet one and a half inches in length. The top of the sceptre has a mound and cross-patée of gold surmounted by a dove with closed wings, enamelled white with a few

THE ENGLISH REGALIA

blue and purple lines upon it. The mound both at the top of the sceptre, and one also at the other end, have champlevé enamels upon them of identical workmanship with that upon the bracelets which, as we have seen, were the work of Sir Robert Vyner, and doubtless the designs upon this sceptre were copied by the royal goldsmith of James II. to match those made for Charles II. Indeed, as they both now are, they agree so closely in colour that I think they have both been re-enamelled more lately than during the seventeenth century. The designs in both these mounds are the double rose, thistle, harp, and fleur-de-lys, separated by a small blue quatrefoil. A similar ornamentation is on the boss at the foot of the sceptre. The eyes, beak, and feet of the dove are of gold.

The fact that the mound at the foot of this sceptre nearly resembles that at the top both in size and ornamentation reminds us that at one time the stems of the orbs themselves were very long, so much so that it is sometimes difficult to say which is orb and which is sceptre. This peculiarity will be seen on reference to some of the sketches showing the early forms of orbs. All the sceptres have large bosses at their lower ends, but in no other instance does it so nearly approach the size of the mound at the top.

BRACELETS.

IN the account of the death of Saul as given by the Amalekite, the 'crown that was upon his head, and the bracelet that was upon his arm,'[1] were taken from him, and bracelets appear to have been at different times used as one of the emblems of sovereignty.

They were worn by Babylonian and Assyrian monarchs, and I am told, in Persia, even at the present time, only the Shah and his sons are allowed to wear them. They were used at the coronation of English sovereigns until lately, and are mentioned in accounts of the coronations of Richard II., Henry VIII., Edward VI., Mary and Elizabeth.

[1] 2 Sam. i. 10.

THE BRACELETS.

THE IVORY SCEPTRE
OF QUEEN MARY OF MODENA.

THE ENGLISH REGALIA

In the list of the regalia made for the coronation of Charles II., by Sir Robert Vyner, mention is made of bracelets, and it is likely that the bracelets now in the Tower are the same as these, but the enamel has undoubtedly been restored at a later date, as it is now identical in colour and preservation with the similar designs which are to be found on what is known as the 'Queen's Ivory Sceptre,' which was made for Mary of Modena.

These bracelets are one and a half inches in breadth, and two and a half in diameter. They are made of solid gold, and are lined with crimson velvet, which is fastened on with red silk drawn through holes pierced in the edges. The edges are marked by raised gold fillets with diagonal lines in blue enamel. The emblems of the three kingdoms and the fleurs-de-lys of France are enamelled on the surface of the bracelet. The designs are cut out of the gold, forming shallow spaces to which the enamel is fixed. This is known as 'champlevé' enamel-work. The double roses are coloured a rich crimson, with little green leaves between the outer petals; the thistles have green cups, pale purple heads and dark green leaves. The harps are pale blue with deep gold strings, and the fleurs-de-lys are a deep rich yellow. These emblems are divided from each other by a dark blue four-petalled flower, with gold centre, and on the fastening of each bracelet are three of these little blue flowers.

MARY OF MODENA'S CIRCLET.

I HAVE shown that in one of the pictures of the coronation procession of Charles II. going to be crowned, he wears only the velvet cap turned up with miniver, and it seems that in many of these processions a cap or circlet not actually a crown was worn, crowns themselves being used on the return journey to Westminster Hall. According to the labels attached to them now in the Tower, we possess both the circlet and the crown that belonged to Mary of Modena, and which she wore in her proceeding to, and on her return from, her coronation. The circlet or diadem, the simpler of the two, is the one she wore first. The crimson velvet cap itself resembles that of Charles II., but has as well a richly jewelled rim or circlet. As it is now, this circlet has along its upper edge a row of large pearls, rising into a point in the front, with a single diamond at its highest point. Beneath this is a rich floral spray, in thick gold open work, elaborately modelled and chased, having large diamonds as leaves and flowers. Beyond this spray on each side are a succession of large rosettes, in open work of gold, with large diamonds in their centres and small diamonds set all round them. This circlet is said to have cost £110,000. There is no record of its having been used by any queen except Mary of Modena, but it undoubtedly differs from the figure of it given by Sandford; but as he shows certain of its peculiarities, such for instance as the gold open-work in clusters, and the single gem in the front, it is just possible that, allowing freely for artistic licence, he intends his figure to represent it even as it is now.

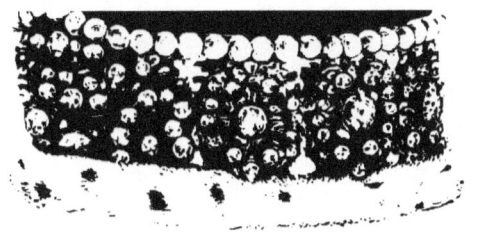

THE CIRCLET OF QUEEN MARY OF MODENA.

THE STATE CROWN OF QUEEN MARY OF MODENA.

MARY OF MODENA'S CROWN.

HE crown that Queen Mary of Modena wore on her return to Westminster Hall after her coronation is figured by Sandford, and it is supposed to be now in the Tower. It is likely that it is the same crown, but there are alterations in the crosses and fleurs-de-lys which surmount the rim, as well as in the cross above the mound; but the main feature of the crown, the row of large diamonds round the rim, is the same in both cases, as are the arches. The only gems used in the crown are diamonds and pearls, and some of the diamonds are very large. I think it is probable that the alterations and improvements which have been made were done for Mary II. The crown has the crimson velvet cap turned up with miniver kept with it.

THE PRINCE OF WALES'S CORONET.

HE eldest son of the sovereigns of England used originally to be called the 'Lord Prince.' Edward I., whose son Edward was born at Carnarvon Castle, invested him with the principality of Wales. This young prince, on the death of his elder brother Alphonso, became heir-apparent to the throne, and since that time the title has been borne by the eldest son of the sovereign. The eldest son of the King or Queen of England is born Duke of Cornwall, and deemed of full age on his birthday, so that he is entitled to the revenues of his Duchy. Since the Union he is also Duke of Rothesay and Seneschal of Scotland from his birth, and at the pleasure of the sovereign he is created by patent Prince of Wales.

The Prince of Wales's coronet is of gold only, and is ornamented with imitation gem clusters and pearls. From the rim rise four crosses-patée and four fleurs-de-lys alternately, and from two opposite crosses rises a single arch, dipping deeply towards the centre. At the top is a mound of gold with imitation pearls, and above this a cross-patée also with pearls. This crown is placed on the Prince's head when he is created Prince of Wales, and is also placed before his seat in the House of Lords when the Queen opens Parliament. Before the Restoration of Charles II. the coronet of the Prince of Wales had no arch, and it was by that king's order that the arch was added with the mound and cross-patée at the top. The coronets of sons, brothers, and uncles of the sovereigns are exactly like that of the Prince of Wales with the exception of the arch, which is not used in their case. The coronets of the princesses of Great Britain are also without the arches, and two of the crosses-patée are replaced by strawberry leaves. The coronet is shown with the crimson velvet cap turned up with miniver with which it is worn.

THE CORONET OF THE PRINCE OF WALES.

SWORDS.

HERE are four swords now kept in the Tower. The largest of these is the Sword of State—a two-handed sword, the length of the blade of which is about thirty-two inches, and the breadth about two inches. The cross of the sword is formed by an arrangement lengthwise of the lion and the unicorn in gilt metal, with a double rose between them. The grip of the sword and the pommel are also of gilt metal. The grip has upon it in raised work designs of the portcullis, fleur-de-lys and harp, and the pommel itself a thistle, orb and other emblems. The upper end of the scabbard has a metal sheathing, gilt, in the form of a portcullis. The lower end has a shoe of gilt metal with designs of portcullis and the lion crest of England upon a crown, and finishes with an orb and cross. The scabbard itself is covered with crimson velvet encircled with gilded metal plates, bearing designs in high relief. The centre plate bears the full royal coat of arms of England, with supporters, and the other plates bear the Tudor badge of the portcullis, the double Tudor rose, the thistle of Scotland, the harp of Ireland, and the fleur-de-lys of France.

Swords are found upon the Great Seals of all our English sovereigns from the time of Edward the Confessor, usually on the reverses, but they have no particular form, and simply mean that the king is a soldier and the head of the army. The sovereign is girded with the sword after being anointed. In Westminster Abbey with the coronation chair is kept a large two-handed sword, said to have belonged to Edward I. It is a state sword of great size, and the form of the handle is evidently the original of the three other swords which are now kept in the Tower. At George the Third's coronation, the Earl Marshal forgot the Sword of State, and one was borrowed from the Lord Mayor to do service instead of it, as fortunately it was not necessary to have the weapon itself, it being only an emblem. The king complained of the neglect to Lord Effingham who was the Deputy Earl Marshal, and he in his confusion replied: 'It is true, sir; but I have taken care that the next coronation shall be regulated in the exactest manner possible.'

There are three other swords besides this state sword—one is called 'Curtana,' one the 'Sword of Justice to the Spirituality,' and the other the 'Sword of Justice to the Temporality,' and these are all now of the same pattern. They are figured by Sir Edward Walker, but the handles that he gives are different from those that now exist. The most curious of these is 'Curtana,' or the 'Sword of Mercy.' It is also known as the sword of Edward the Confessor, and it was formerly the privilege of

THE ENGLISH REGALIA

the Earls of Chester to carry it before the king. Its point is blunt, cut off square, but in Sir Edward Walker's account it is shown jagged. This blunted point is supposed to be typical of the quality of mercy. The handles of the three swords are of a simple pattern, all gilded; the pommels being thick octagonal plates with circular centres. The scabbards are covered with crimson velvet ornamented with a running scroll in gold braid. The length of 'Curtana' is about thirty-two inches, and the breadth of the blade two inches. The other two swords are a little longer, and the breadth of their blades a little less, and they are both pointed in the usual manner.

SPURS.

IN the list of the regalia made for Charles II., and drawn out in 1685 in preparation for the coronation of James II., mention is made of a pair of golden spurs. They are figured both in Sir Edward Walker's account of the coronation of Charles II., and in Sandford's account of the coronation of James II., and appear to be the same now as they were then, with the exception of the straps and buckles. They were most probably made by Sir Robert Vyner, and are of the kind known as 'prick' spurs, as they do not end in a rowel, but in a sharp point projecting from a conventional flower. They are of solid gold, richly chased in flowing patterns, and have straps of crimson velvet embroidered in gold. They are known as St. George's spurs, and are of course the emblem of knighthood and chivalry, and with the sword help to mark the military character of the sovereign. At the coronation these spurs are presented to the sovereign, and immediately deposited on the altar, being afterwards redeemed by the payment of some handsome fee. This procedure, indeed, takes place with most of the articles used at the coronation, one after the other.

In former days, no one was allowed to enter a sacred edifice with

ST. GEORGE'S SPURS.

THE SWORD OF STATE.　　　　　　　　　THE SWORD "CURTANA."

THE ENGLISH REGALIA

military arms upon him. These were generally left with one of the attendants at the door or in the porch, while their owner went inside to pray. When the prayers were finished and the soldier came out again, he had to redeem his accoutrements with such money as he had available, and 'spur money' had always to be taken into consideration when an armed knight went to his devotions.

QUEEN VICTORIA'S STATE CROWN.

THIS beautiful piece of jewellery was made by Rundell and Bridge in 1838. Many of the gems in it are old ones reset, and many of them are new. The entire weight of the crown is 39 oz. 5 dwt. It consists of a circlet of open work in silver, bearing in the front the great sapphire from the crown of Charles II. which was bequeathed to George III. by Cardinal York, with other Stuart treasure. At one end this gem is partly pierced. It is not a thick stone, but it is a fine colour. Opposite to the large sapphire is one of smaller size. The remainder of the rim is filled in with rich jewel clusters, having alternately sapphires and emeralds in their centres, enclosed in ornamental borders thickly set with diamonds. These clusters are separated from each other by trefoil designs also thickly set with diamonds. The rim is bordered above and below with bands of large pearls, 129 in the lower row, and 112 in the upper. Above the rim are shallow festoons of diamonds, caught up between the larger ornaments by points of emeralds encircled with diamonds, and a large pearl above each. On these festoons are set alternately eight crosses-patée and eight fleurs-de-lys of silver set with gems. The crosses-patée are thickly set with brilliants and have each an emerald in the centre, except that in the front of the crown, which contains the most remarkable jewel belonging to the regalia. This is a large spinel ruby of irregular drop-like form, measuring about two inches in length, and is highly polished on what is probably its natural surface, or nearly so. Its irregular outline makes it possible to recognise the place that it has formerly occupied in the older state crowns, and it seems always to have been given the place of honour. It is pierced after an Oriental fashion, and the top of the piercing is filled with a supplementary ruby set in gold. Don Pedro, King of Castile, in 1367 murdered the King of Granada for the sake of his jewels, one of which was this stone, and Don Pedro is said to have given it to Edward the Black Prince after the battle of Najera, near Vittoria, in the same year. After this, it is said to have been worn by Henry the Fifth in his crown at Agincourt in 1415, when it is recorded that the king's life was saved from the attack of the Duc D'Alençon, because of the protection afforded him by his crown, a portion of which, however, was broken off. It may be confidently predicted that such a risk of destruction is not very likely to happen again to the great ruby.

In the centre of each of the very ornamental fleurs-de-lys is a ruby, and all the rest of the ornamentation on them is composed of rose

THE ENGLISH REGALIA

diamonds, large and small. From each of the crosses-patée, the upper corners of which have each a large pearl upon them, rises an arch of silver worked into a design of oak leaves and acorn cups. These leaves and cups are all closely encrusted with a mass of large and small diamonds, rose, brilliant, and table cut; the acorns themselves being formed of beautiful drop-shaped pearls of large size. From the four points of intersection of the arches at the top of the crown depend large egg-shaped pearls. From the centre of the arches, which slope slightly upwards, springs a mound with a cross-patée above it. The mound is ornamented all over with close lines of brilliant diamonds, and the fillet which encircles it, and the arch which crosses over it, are both ornamented with one line of large rose-cut diamonds set closely together. The cross-patée at the top has in the centre a large sapphire of magnificent colour set openly. The outer lines of the arms of the cross are marked by a row of small diamonds close together, and in the centre of each arm is a large diamond, the remaining spaces being filled with more small diamonds. The large sapphire in the centre of this cross is said to have come out of the ring of Edward the Confessor, which was buried with him in his shrine at Westminster, and the possession of it is supposed to give to the owner the power of curing the cramp. If this be indeed the stone which belonged to St. Edward, it was probably recut in its present form of a 'rose' for Charles II., even if not since his time.

Not counting the large ruby or the large sapphire, this crown contains—
- four rubies,
- eleven emeralds,
- sixteen sapphires,
- two hundred and seventy-seven pearls,
- two thousand seven hundred and eighty-three diamonds.

The large ruby has been valued at £110,000.

When this crown has to take a journey, it is provided with a little box, lined with white velvet, and having a sliding drawer at the bottom with a boss on which the crown fits closely, so that it is safe from slipping. The velvet cap turned up with miniver, with which it is worn, is kept with it.

THE MACES, BANQUETING PLATE, Etc.

HE Mace was originally a weapon used by cavalry soldiers, and the general shape of the ancient maces—a short handle with a broad head—is retained in the ornamental maces used at our coronations, in Parliament, by the mayors of towns, and in other cognate cases. The crowned mace indicates the delegation of royal authority, and is a mark of dignity, used on ceremonial occasions, and carried in procession by chosen officials. A policeman's staff is really a small mace, and was until lately surmounted by a crown.

FIG. 57.—THE SERJEANTS-AT-ARMS CARRYING THEIR MACES. FROM THE CORONATION PROCESSION OF CHARLES II. AFTER WENCESLAUS HOLLAR.

The royal maces are carried at coronations by the serjeants-at-arms, originally a corps of twenty-four knights, or gentlemen higher than that degree, said to have been instituted by Richard I., whose duty it was to be in attendance on the king's person. They were mounted at the coronation of Charles II. (fig. 57), but on foot at that of James II.

There are several maces in the Tower, the oldest and finest of which are two that were most likely made by Sir Robert Vyner for Charles II., whose initials are upon them. They are of silver gilt, and measure a little over four feet in length.

The head of each of these maces, which have served as models to the other royal maces, consists of a massive rounded bowl, divided externally into four compartments, each bearing a crown flanked by the initials C. R., and under the crowns are the emblems of the three kingdoms, the rose, thistle, harp, and fleur-de-lys, in high repoussé-work finished with chasing. The compartments are marked out by ornamental scroll divisions, on each of which is a conventional female figure.

In many instances these bowls at the top of maces were made to unscrew, and were used as drinking-cups, being provided with a short foot as well—the ornamental crown at the top also being removable.

THE ENGLISH REGALIA

Above this is a crown, the rim of which, widening slightly outwards, bears eight small crosses-patée, and eight small fleurs-de-lys, raised on points, and with pearl points between each. From alternate crosses-patée rise two arches, dipping at the point of intersection, with a row of 'pearls' along the centre of each.

From the point of intersection rises a large orb with fillet round the thickest part of it, and an arch crossing it at the top. On the top of the mound is a cross-patée with a 'pearl' in the centre, and also one at each extremity of the three upper arms.

The handle of the mace is chased and ornamented with a graceful design of superimposed arches, in each of which is either a rose or a thistle. It is divided into three divisions by two broad knops of oblate form, repoussés and chased in a simple design. The upper of these divisions is much the smallest, and is further decorated with three ornamental brackets of open tracery with masks and curves richly designed. The foot widens out into a rounded boss repoussé and chased in a pattern resembling that of the smaller knops, but more ornamentally treated and differently proportioned, and the foot has another smaller thickening decorated in the same way.

The remaining maces are all made on the same plan, but they are larger, and differ in the details of the ornamentation, and also in the initials of the sovereign for whom they were made—James II., William and Mary, or one of the Georges.

The fine christening font of silver gilt was made for Charles II. It has a high foot and richly repoussé stand. It is used, I am told, only for the christening of the heir-apparent; and is a finely-worked specimen of English plate.

The great maundy dish is also kept in the Tower. It is silver gilt, and has engraved in the centre the royal coat of arms within the garter, and the initials of William and Mary. From this dish the alms are distributed on Maundy Thursday.

The sacramental flagon and repoussé altar-dish both bear the monogram of William and Mary.

With these exceptions, all the royal plate now in the Tower really belongs to the table furniture of the state banquet, which used to be held in Westminster Hall after the coronation, but has been discontinued since the coronation of George IV. The pieces are chiefly great salt-cellars, the most important being that of Elizabeth, which is specially described; the next finest being a set of seven made for Charles II., with a mounted knight at the top; then there are four of massive form, also made for Charles, all these being worked in high repoussé and richly chased, of silver gilt. There are a dozen salt-spoons with twisted stalk handles.

The curious gold salt-cellar, fashioned like a square tower with four

THE ENGLISH REGALIA

corner turrets, a large turret rising from the centre, and topped by a crown, was presented to the Crown by the city of Exeter. It is studded in places with gems, especially one fine emerald, and is generally supposed to represent the White Tower, but the authority for this does not appear.

The magnificent wine fountain was given to Charles II. by the Corporation of Plymouth. The bowl part is divided into several shallow basins, and a thick ornamental column with rich modelling rises in the centre, finishing with a figure-group at the top. It is a splendid piece of plate, and well and largely designed, the actual workmanship also being excellent.

There are also with the regalia proper some silver-gilt tankards of foreign make, and in a side-case the state silver trumpets with their heavily embroidered falls, and in the window-cases the official copies of the Orders of the Empire.

THE CORONATION BOOK.

IT seems rather curious that, considering the importance of the coronation oath, we have no official Bible on which it is to be taken. The Book has, at all events since the time of Henry VIII., been provided anew at each coronation, and indeed it is probable that if we had possessed a fine book—possibly covered with gold and gems—it would have been destroyed in 1649 with the rest of the regalia.

The coronation oath is very old, and is traced back a long way. Lingard, in his history of the Anglo-Saxon Church, says it is referable to Anthenius, Patriarch of Constantinople, who refused to crown Anastasius until he had sworn to make no change in the established religion. This was in the fifth century; but it is most probable that, long before, there was some form of oath administered to rulers, by virtue of which their protection of the religion of their subjects was secured.

In the library of the Society of Antiquaries at Burlington House, in one of the scrap-books, is a drawing by Vertue of a curious old book said to have been that on which our kings from Henry I. to Henry VIII. took their coronation oath.

This same book is now in the manuscript department of the British Museum, and, apart from its historical interest, it has the distinction of being one of the very few decorative bindings of English workmanship of the twelfth century now existing.

It is a vellum manuscript of extracts from the Gospels in Latin, with interlinear Saxon version, and it also contains all the Gospel of St. John except some missing pages, and a few other extracts. Inside the book are several notes concerning its history: one signed by John Ives at 'Yarmouth, St. Luke's Day 1772,' says it 'appears to be the original book on which our Kings and Queens took their coronation oath before the Reformation.' Powell, in the *Repertory of Records*, 1631, at page 123 mentions 'a little booke with a crucifix,' and says it is preserved in the chest of the King's Remembrancer at the Exchequer.

Mr. Thomas Madox, author of the *History of the Exchequer*, considered that it was the book formerly belonging to the Exchequer, which was mentioned by Powell. It was shown to Mr. Madox by ' Mr. Thomas Palgrave,' who owned it in the eighteenth century; but how it left the 'chest of the King's Remembrancer at the Exchequer' there is nothing to show. Early in the present century it belonged to Mr. Thomas Astle, Keeper of the Records in the Tower, and on his death, with the rest of

THE ENGLISH REGALIA

his library, it became the property by purchase of the Marquis of Buckingham. Although a beautiful Gothic room had been built at Stowe in which to keep this library, it was all sold in 1849 to Lord Ashburnham. From Lord Ashburnham the 'Stowe' library was purchased by the Trustees of the British Museum in 1883, and so this little book became once more national property, and is not likely to leave its present guardianship.

It is covered with thick wooden boards three-quarters of an inch thick, covered with deer-skin. On the lower cover is a sunk panel, and in this is a figure of our Lord, finely modelled and chased. The figure shows remains of old gilding, and the workmanship is excellent. The corners are protected by corner-pieces of gilt metal, each with a boss and a design of a fleur-de-lys within a circle stamped upon them, and there is an old clasp (fig. 58).

FIG. 58.—THE 'CORONATION BOOK' OF HENRY I.

The figure of our Saviour and the clasp are probably contemporary with the rest of the binding and the manuscript itself, but the corner-pieces are apparently a subsequent addition.

As far as can be ascertained from pictures of recent coronations, the Bible upon which the oath has been taken was covered in dark blue velvet with gilt clasps, centre-pieces, and corners. That used by Queen Victoria was in 1883 the property of the Rev. J. H. Sumner, Rector of Buriton, Hants. It came to him from his father, the Bishop of Winchester, to whom it was given after the coronation.

THE KOH-I-NOOR.

THE Koh-i-noor seems to have been originally found in the Golconda diamond-mines in the Deccan, and when the Mogul princes extended their rule to this district the prime minister of the king of Golconda conspired with Shah Jehaun against his master, and plotted to obtain possession of the stone. Between them, the prime minister and the Mogul Emperor contrived eventually to succeed in their designs, and the jewel passed from Golconda to Delhi. The Emperor Aurengzebe, the son of Jehaun, allowed the French traveller Tavernier to see the gem in 1665, and he was permitted to examine it carefully in the presence of the Emperor himself. It was kept at Delhi until 1739, when it was captured by Nadir Shah, the king of Persia, who carried it away to Korassan. It is said that when Nadir Shah took possession of Delhi Mohammed Shah endeavoured to hide the great diamond, but a lady of Mohammed's harem told Nadir Shah that it was hidden in Mohammed's turban, and, at a festival, the Persian king offered Mohammed an Oriental form of compliment, consisting of an exchange of turbans, and by this device he obtained possession of the jewel. Nadir Shah was presently assassinated, but among his Afghan guard was a certain Ahmed Shah, who had access to his treasure. This chieftain with his fellow-Afghans managed to escape into their own country, carrying the stone with them.

Ahmed eventually became the ruler at Cabul, and founded the Doorânnee monarchy. One of Ahmed's descendants, Shah Shuja, wore the gem set as an armlet, probably in the same setting as is now in the Tower, on the occasion of the embassy of Mr. Elphinstone to Peshâwur, and, on his expulsion from Cabul shortly afterwards, he managed to carry the diamond away with him. Shah Shuja found a refuge with the Sikh ruler Runjeet Singh at Lahore, who, in return for his hospitality, insisted upon the gem being given to him, and he obtained possession of it in 1813. Dhuleep Singh duly inherited the gem, and it belonged to him until 1849 when the East India Company annexed Lahore, and it was presented by them to the Queen of England, and was sent to her by Lord Dalhousie under the care of Major Mackeson, reaching this country in 1850. It was exhibited in the Great Exhibition of 1851, and was then valued at £140,000.

When the stone was first in the possession of Shah Jehaun it was uncut, and is said to have weighed nearly eight hundred carats. It was sent by Jehaun to a Venetian lapidary, Ortensio Borgio, to be cut, but

THE ENGLISH REGALIA

it was supposed that he spoilt it, and the Sultan made him pay ten thousand rupees as a punishment. Borgio not only cut the stone badly, but very greatly reduced its weight. When brought to Europe it only weighed one hundred and eighty-six and one-sixteenth carats. Its shape when it came here was that of a truncated cone with a large number of small facets, nearly resembling, indeed, the shape of a mountain in miniature. This manner of cutting a diamond is by no means calculated to show its brilliancy to the greatest advantage; and the Prince Consort took counsel with many lapidaries and men of science, especially Sir David Brewster, with a view to finding out not only the best manner of having it recut, but also to decide the difficult question as to who should be intrusted with the delicate task. After much deliberation, the form of a regularly cut brilliant was decided upon, and the work was given to Messrs. Coster of Amsterdam, who sent over here to have it executed —the actual cutter being Herr Voorsanger, of Amsterdam.

The cutting was commenced on 6th July 1852—according to some authorities by the Prince Consort himself, and according to others by the Duke of Wellington, so it is probable that both these gentlemen were present. The weight after the cutting was reduced to one hundred and six and one-sixteenth carats. The form that the diamond was cut in has been adversely criticised because of the shallowness of the stone; but the only alternative form would appear to have been that which the stone already possessed, which might possibly have been to some extent improved, but never could have been so brilliant as the form adopted. The great loss of weight is to some extent accounted for by the fact that Herr Voorsanger found several flaws—one especially big one—that he considered it necessary to cut away. The stone is now worn by her Majesty as a brooch, and is kept at Windsor; and although the original setting is deposited in the Tower with the rest of the regalia, the jewel itself is her Majesty's private property, which is quite in accordance with the Indian superstition concerning it, which is that its ownership takes with it the sovereignty of Hindostan.

The armlet of Shah Shuja, which is most likely the one in the Tower, held three gems, now replaced by models—the Koh-i-noor in the centre with two drop-shaped diamonds at each side of it, in a setting of gold richly enamelled (fig. 59). The enamels which show upon the front are green and white, but those at the back of the stone are red, blue, green and white in beautiful Indian patterns. Then, after two gold attachments, come thick strands of crimson silk, brought together with a twist of gold

FIG. 59.—THE ARMLET OF SHAH SHUJA CONTAINING THE KOH-I-NOOR.

THE ENGLISH REGALIA

thread, and ending in a tassel of large pearls each surmounted by a ruby bead. The armlet is excellently arranged over a looking-glass, so that the enamels at the back of the stone can be well seen.

The model of the Koh-i-noor shows the manner of its cutting when it was brought over in 1850.

ST. EDWARD'S CHAIR.

ST. EDWARD'S Chair may be considered to be part of the regalia of England, and since it has been in this country its home has always been in Westminster Abbey. It was brought from Scotland by Edward I. in 1296, after his defeat of John Baliol. All our kings since that time have been crowned upon it at Westminster, except Mary I.; and when Cromwell was installed Lord Protector, it was taken to Westminster Hall for him. The seat holds 'Jacob's stone,' twenty-two inches long, eleven broad, and about six in depth, on which tradition says the patriarch Jacob slept in the plain of Luz. Holinshed in his *Historie of Scotland* gives a curious history of a Greek noble, Gathelus, son of Cecrops, the builder of Athens. Gathelus, being of a turbulent and wandering disposition, went from Greece into Egypt with several companions, 'anno mundi 2416.' Here he made friends with Pharao the king, and eventually married his daughter Scota—from whom it is said the name of Scotia is derived.

On the death of Pharao, Gathelus, not agreeing with his successors, left Egypt and settled at Compostella, where he was 'intituled by the name of king,' and 'sat upon his marble stone in Brigantia.' The two sons of Gathelus, however, not liking Spain, migrated to an island 'lying north ouer agaynst Spayne,' and landed at 'Dundalke,' the island being called 'Hibernia,' after one of them whose name was Hyberus.

The stone they are supposed to have brought with them, and it is described as being 'in fashion like a seate or chayre, having a fatall destinie, as the Scottes say, following it, that wheresoever it shoulde be founde, there shoulde the Scottish men raigne and haue the supreme gouernance. Hereof it came to passe that first in Spaine, after in Irelande, and then in Scotlande, the kings which ruled ouer the Scottish men receyued the crowne sitting upon that stone, untill the time of Robert the First, king of Scotlande.' It is said to have been taken to Ireland about 700 B.C. by Simon Brech, king of Scots. Thence it was taken to Scotland by King Fergus, about 330 B.C., and in 850 A.D. it was placed in the Abbey of Scone by King Kenneth. He found it at Dunstaffnage, a royal Scottish castle, the sandstone of which, by the bye, has a very near resemblance to the stone itself; in fact, it is undoubtedly, geologically speaking, the same dull reddish sandstone. It must not be forgotten that the Mohammedans say Jacob's stone is

THE ENGLISH REGALIA

now preserved at Jerusalem, and that consequently our story is the wrong one. King Kenneth had it enclosed in a wooden chair, of which the present one is a copy made for Edward I., and particulars concerning it are to be found in his Wardrobe Accounts (fig. 60). It was originally gilded, painted, and inlaid in places with glass mosaics, traces of which can still be seen on a careful examination, especially on the back of the chair. It was dedicated by Edward I. to St. Edward the Confessor in 1297, and the part of the Abbey in which it is kept is still known as St. Edward's Chapel. Edward had an engraved plate inserted in the stone, and on it the legend—

'Ni fallat fatum, Scoti hunc quoqunque locatum
Inveniunt lapidem regnare tenentur ibidem';

which may be translated—

FIG. 60.—ST. EDWARD'S CHAIR.

'Except old saws do fail, and wizards' wits be blind,
The Scots in place must reign where they this stone shall find.'

This plate is now gone, but a space remains to mark the place to which it was formerly attached. A cross is cut upon the stone, and it has old handles at the ends. Another superstition concerning it was that it was said to groan or speak whenever any of the monarchs of the Scythian race seated themselves upon it; and this must have been known to Hector Boece, who notes a fuller version of the old Scoto-Irish prophecy which, being translated, says—

'Unless the fixed decrees of fate give way
The Scots shall govern and the sceptre sway,
Where'er this stone they find, and its dread sound obey.'

The four lions upon which the chair rests are gilded, and one of them had a new face put upon him for the coronation of George IV. For the coronation ceremony itself the chair is carefully covered with cloth of gold. Its appearance, when prepared for the coronation, shows admirably in Sir George Hayter's beautiful picture of the coronation of Queen Victoria, in which the Queen is seen just after she has been crowned, holding in her right hand the royal sceptre with the cross, and in her left the sceptre with the dove, and wearing the 'Colobium Sindonis,' stole, dalmatic, and mantle. She also has a high footstool, and the Gothic pinnacles at the top of the chair were apparently restored for the occasion (fig. 61).

Sacred stones have been used in many countries and at many times as seats for the coronation ceremonies of kings; and although the stone which has been used in England since the time of Edward I. for this

THE ENGLISH REGALIA

purpose came, as we have seen, from Scotland, we possess at Kingston an old piece of what was most likely a holy Druidical stone of our own altogether. This stone was used for the coronation of some of our Saxon kings certainly, and, probably enough, for more of them than is recorded. As early as the reign of Edred, in 946, in a charter, mention is made of Kingston as the royal town in which the coronation is usually performed, and the fact of the stone being there gives the place its name.

During the tenth and eleventh centuries seven of our kings are known to have been crowned at Kingston, and the Saxon monarchs had a palace there, as nearly as can be ascertained, on the spot where the stone now is. The stone itself resembles the stones of the Druids at

FIG. 61.—QUEEN VICTORIA SEATED IN ST. EDWARD'S CHAIR.

FIG. 62.—THE KINGSTON CORONATION STONE.

Stonehenge, and it is extremely likely to have had some especially sacred character (fig. 62).

It is now resting on a septangular block of stone enclosed within an iron railing, with a pilaster of stone at each of the seven corners. The arrangement and design of the railing and pillars is excellent, and under each of the columns is a penny of one of the kings that were certainly crowned there.

INDEX

ÆTHELRED II., Sceptre of, 19.
Æthelstan, Crowns of, 21.
Agincourt, Battle of, 3, 50.
Ahmed Shah, 57.
Alençon, Duc d', 3, 50.
Alfonso, Prince, 46.
Alfred, King, Crown of, 4, 21.
Amherst of Hackney, Lord, vii, 13, 24, 25.
Ampulla, 28.
Anastasius, Emperor, 55.
Anointing, Directions for, 28.
Antiquaries, Society of, 30, 55.
Archæologia, 4.
Arches, Crowns with, 21, 23, 24, 25, 26.
Ashburnham, Earl of, 56.
Astle, Mr. Thomas, 55.
Athenius, Patriarch of Constantinople, 55.
Aurengzebe, Emperor, 57.

BAGFORD COLLECTION, 12.
Baliol, John, King of Scotland, 25, 60.
Bannockburn, 25.
Banqueting Plate at the Tower, 52.
Biddulph, Sir Michael A. S., v.
Blood, Colonel, 24.
Bodleian Library, Oxford, 1.
Borgio, Ortensio, 57.
Bracelets, 42.
Bray, Sir Reginald, 3.
Brech, Simon, King of Scots, 60.
Brewster, Sir David, 58.
British Museum, Coronation authorities at the, 1.
—— —— Bagford Collection at the, 12.
—— —— Golden cup of Henry VI. at the, 26.
—— —— Ivory diptych at the, 17.
—— —— Queen Elizabeth's enamelled book at the, 13.
Bruce, Robert, King of Scotland, 25.
Buckingham, Duke of, 3.
—— Marquis of, 56.

CANTERBURY, Archbishop of, 28.
Canute, Crown of, 21.
—— Sceptre of, 19.
Castile, Pedro, King of, 50.
Chaffers, Mr. William, vi, 30.

Charles, Prince of Wales, 3.
—— I., Sale of treasure by, 3, 4.
—— —— Ring of, 26.
—— II., Coronation of, 5.
—— —— Orb of, 37.
—— —— Sceptre of, 35, 38.
—— —— State Crown of, 25.
—— —— Vestments of, 8.
Chrisma, or Holy Cream, 28.
Christening font at the Tower, 53.
Circlet of Queen Mary of Modena, 44.
Colobium Sindonis of Queen Victoria, 1, 14, 15.
Commonwealth, 4.
Consort, the Prince, 58.
Cornwall, Duke of, 46.
Coronation, Order of, 1.
—— Book, 55.
—— Ring, 26.
—— Spoon, 30.
Coronet of the Prince of Wales, 46.
Coster, of Amsterdam, 58.
Cripps, Mr. W., 30.
Cromwell, 11, 60.
Cross, Crowns with, 23, 24, 25.
—— Orbs with, 17.
—— Sceptres with, 19, 35, 36.
Crown of Queen Mary of Modena, 45.
—— of Scotland, 26.
Crowns, 21.
'Curtana,' 47.

DALHOUSIE, Lord, 57.
Dalmatic of Charles II., 8.
—— of James II., 11.
—— of Queen Victoria, 15.
Dhuleep Singh, Maharajah, 57.
Dove, Orb with, 17.
—— Sceptres with, 20, 38, 39.
Dunnottar Castle, 25.
Dunstaffnage, Castle of, 60.

EDINBURGH CASTLE, 25, 26.
Edith, Queen, Crown of, 4.
Edward the Confessor, Crown of, 21.
—— —— Orb of, 17.
—— —— Ring of, 51.
—— —— Sceptres of, 19.

63

THE ENGLISH REGALIA

Edward I., Coronation Chair of, 60.
—— — Crown of, 23.
—— — Stole of, 14.
—— III., Sceptre of, 20.
—— IV., Crown of, 23.
—— the Black Prince, 50.
Effingham, Earl of, 47.
Elizabeth, Queen, Salt-cellar of, 32.
Elphinstone, Embassy of Mr., 57.
Exeter, Salt-cellar presented by city of, 54.

Fergus, King of Scotland, 60.
Fleurs-de-lys, Crowns with, 21, 22, 23, 24, 25, 26.
—— Sceptres with, 19, 20.
Frederick III., Emperor, Golden Bulla of, 14.

Gathelus, 60.
George III., 26.
—— IV., State Crown of, 25.
Golconda Mines, 57.
Granada, King of, 50.
Griggs, Mr. William, v.

Harold II., Coronation of, 37.
—— Crown of, 22.
—— Sceptre of, 20.
Hayter, Sir George, 61.
Henry I., Crowns of, 22.
—— — Orb of, 17.
—— III., Orbs of, 17.
—— — Sceptre of, 20.
—— IV., Sceptre of, 20.
—— V., at Agincourt, 3, 50.
—— VI., Crown of, 23.
—— — Golden enamelled cup of, 26.
—— VII., at Bosworth, 3.
—— — Crowns of, 23.
—— — Orb of, 17.
—— VIII., Crown of, 24.
—— — Orb of, 18.
Holinshed, 60.
Holland, Royal Treasure pawned to, 3.
Hollar, Wenceslaus, 52.
Hyberus, 60.

Inventories of Regalia, etc., 4, etc.
Ivory Rod of Queen Mary of Modena, 41.

Jackson, Mr. C. J., 30.
Jacob's Stone, 60.
James II., Sceptre of, 35.
—— State Crown of, 25.
—— Vestments of, 9, etc.
—— V., King of Scotland, 25.

Jehaun, Shah, 57.
Jones, Mr. W., vi, 28, 30.

Keeper of the Regalia, first mention of the, 3.
Kenneth, King of Scotland, 60.
Kingston Stone, 62.
Koh-i-noor, 57.

Legg, Dr. J. Wickham, vi.
Liber Regalis, 1.

Maces, 52.
Mackeson, Major, 57.
Madox, Mr. Thomas, 55.
Mantle of Charles II., 9.
—— of James II., 9.
—— of Queen Victoria, 16.
Mary I., 11, 60.
—— II., Orb of, 40.
—— — Sceptre of, 39.
—— of Modena, Queen, Circlet of, 11, 44.
—— —— Ivory Rod of, 41.
—— —— Sceptre of, 36.
—— —— State Crown of, 45.
—— Queen of Scots, 25.
—— the Virgin, 28.
Maundy Dish at the Tower, 53.
Methven, 25.
Middleton, Sir Frederick D., v.
Mildmay, Sir Harry, 4.
Mohammed Shah, 57.
Monstrance, Sceptre with, 20.

Nadir Shah, 57.
Najera, battle of, 50.
Nayler, Sir George, vi, 12, 25.

Ogilvy, John, vi, 8.
Orb, the larger, 37.
—— the smaller, 40.
Orbs, 17.

Palgrave, Mr. Thomas, 55.
Pearls, Crowns with, 21, 22.
—— Sceptres with, 19, 20.
Pedro, King of Castile, 50.
Pharao, King of Egypt, 60.
Plymouth, Wine Fountain given by the town of, 54.
Powell's *Repertory of Records*, 55.
'Protestant Joy,' 3.

Regalia, Keeper of the, 3.
Richard I., Orb of, 17.

INDEX

Richard III. at Bosworth, 3.
Richmond, Earl of, 3.
Ring, the Coronation, 26.
Robert I., King of Scotland, 60.
Royle, Mr. Arnold, vi.
Ruby in Queen Victoria's State Crown, 50.
Ruding, Rev. Rogers, vii.
Rundell and Bridge, 50.
Runjeet Singh, 57.
Rymer's *Fœdera*, vi.

St. Armand, Mr. James, 28.
St. Edward's Chair, 60.
—— Crown, 34.
—— Staff, 41.
—— Chapel, 61.
St. George's Spurs, 48.
St. Thomas of Canterbury, 28.
Salt-cellar of Queen Elizabeth, 32.
Salt-cellar presented by the city of Exeter, 54.
Sandford, Francis, vi, 10, 12, 32, 34, 35, 36, 38, 39, 40.
Sandwich, Earl of, 6.
Sapphires in Queen Victoria's State Crown, 50, 51.
Saul, 42.
Sceptres, 19.
—— with Cross, 35, 36.
—— with Dove, 20, 38, 39.
—— with Fleurs-de-lys, 19, 20.
—— with Pearls, 19, 20.
Scone, Abbey of, 60.
Scota, daughter of Pharao, King of Egypt, 60.
Scott, Sir Walter, 25.
Scottish Crown, 26.
Scottish Regalia, 25.
Serjeants-at-Arms, 52.
Shaw, Mr. Henry, 30.
Shuja, Shah, 57.
Spain, war with, 3.
Spoon, the Coronation, 30.
Spurs, 48.
Stanley, Lord, at Bosworth, 3.
State Crowns, 24, 25.
State Swords, 47.

Stephanoff, drawings by, 12.
Stephen, Crown of, 22.
Stole of Charles II., 8.
—— of James II., 12.
—— of Queen Victoria, 16.
Stonehenge, 62.
Stowe, library at, 56.
Swords, 47.
Sumner, Rev. J. H., 56.
Surcoat of James II., 11.

Talbott, Sir Gilbert, 6.
Tassels on Crowns, 21, 22.
Tavernier, 57.
Thomas, St., of Canterbury, 28.
Tower of London, 3.

Vertue, drawing by, 55.
Vestments of Charles II., 8.
—— of James II., 9, etc.
—— of Queen Victoria, 14, etc.
Victoria, Queen, State Crown of, 50.
—— —— Vestments of, 14, etc.
Voorsanger, Herr, 58.
Vyner, Sir Robert, 6, 7, 18, 29, 31, 34, 37, 41, 42, 48.

Wales, Coronet of the Prince of, 46.
Walker, Sir Edward, vi, 7, 10, 12, 24, 34, 35, 37, 38, 47, 48.
Wellington, Duke of, 58.
Westminster Abbey, muniment room at, 1.
—— —— Treasury at, 3.
William I., Crowns of, 22.
—— Orb of, 17.
—— II., Crown of, 22.
—— IV., State Crown of, 25.
—— and Mary, Coronation of, 12.
Winchester, Bishop of, 56.
Wine Fountain at the Tower, 54.
Wyon, Mr. Alfred B., vi.
—— Mr. Allan, vi.

York, Cardinal, 26, 50.

www.ingramcontent.com/pod-product-compliance
Lightning Source LLC
Chambersburg PA
CBHW020152170426
43199CB00010B/1003